(THE JAPANESE MOVIE:)

AN ILLUSTRATED HISTORY

by DONALD RICHIE

 KODANSHA INTERNATIONAL LTD.: PUBLISHERS

TOKYO, JAPAN   PALO ALTO, CALIFORNIA, U. S. A.

To the
memory of the
late
tokutaro Osawa,
who began
and sustained
my interest

DISTRIBUTORS:

British Commonwealth (excluding Canada and the Far East)
WARD LOCK & COMPANY LTD.
London

France
HACHETTE — LIBRAIRIE ETRANGERE
Paris

Continental Europe (excluding France)
BOXERBOOKS, INC.
Zurich

The Far East
JAPAN PUBLICATIONS TRADING COMPANY
C.P.O. Box 722, Tokyo

Published by Kodansha International Ltd., 3-19, Otowa-cho, Bunkyo-ku, Tokyo, Japan
and Kodansha International/usa, Ltd., 577 College Avenue, Palo Alto, California 94306.
Copyright in Japan, 1966, by Kodansha International Ltd. All rights reserved. Printed in
Japan.

Library of Congress Catalog Card No. 66-12172

First edition, 1966
Second printing, 1966

ACKNOWLEDGEMENTS

IN WRITING *this "social history" of the Japanese cinema, I have been indebted to a number of people. First, I remain grateful to Joseph Anderson, with whom I wrote* The Japanese Film. *That many of his ideas have become mine will be apparent to those who know both volumes. Second, I have relied greatly on Toyoji Kuroda and his staff at UniJapan Film, particularly Osamu Sakamoto, who has been of the greatest assistance to me. Third, to a number of critics who are not to be blamed for the use I have made of their ideas, but who must also be gratefully acknowledged; foremost among these would be Siegfried Kracauer, Jean Debrix, and Vernon Young.*

I am also grateful to Junnichi Tanaka, Japan's foremost film historian, and to Shunsai Matsuda, one of the few who makes his business the Japanese classic cinema. Finally, I am grateful to all of those who made possible the many stills in this volume, credit for which is given following each entry in the index of this book.

DONALD RICHIE
1965

PREFACE

THE HISTORY of the film in Japan has been a long and interesting one. That people in other countries only know the Japanese film since Kurosawa's *Rashomon*, Mizoguchi's *Ugetsu*, and my own *Gate of Hell* is unfortunate—they came in when the picture was half over, so to speak. One of the reasons, then, that I welcome this new book is that it includes not only a history of this time which even to me has begun to seem long ago, but that so very many pictures are included—that it is, indeed, a pictorial history. Further, pictures and text covering the span of almost seventy years combine to recreate the nearest thing we have to the films themselves. This is a social history, an esthetic history, the story of the Japanese film fulfilling itself and in its turn reflecting the history of our country and our people. I am proud that I had my own part in creating this history, and I am delighted that this history has now come alive again in this book.

TEINOSUKE KINUGASA

THE JAPANESE MOVIE:
an illustrated history

THE LATTER decades of the nineteenth century were, in Japan even more than elsewhere, an era of commercial expansion and what was then known as progress. After nearly three hundred years of self-enforced seclusion, Japan (having fallen asleep under Elizabeth) suddenly awoke in the reign of Victoria and busied itself lest it miss entirely this new age of trade, treaties, and invention. Things Western became for a time à la mode, and only the fear of a major conflagration kept the people of Nara from going through with their planned ritual burning of the great but insufferably old-fashioned five-tiered Kofuku-ji pagoda. Instead of such wholesale destruction, phallic stones were selectively uprooted, pants were put on the workmen, mixed bathing was discouraged, a war with China was begun and successfully concluded, and a number of Western innovations were introduced. Among these were Pittsburgh gold watches, derbies, bustles (originally worn in front due to a misunderstanding), railroad engines, and the movies.

In the middle decades of the century, a Frenchman, Etienne-Jules Marey, and an Englishman, Edweard Muybridge, had been experimenting with what later became the motion picture. Bernard Shaw knew the former and spoke of him as "the man who used to drop cats out of the window and photograph them as they fell." Word of their interesting experiments came to Thomas Edison, often erroneously called the inventor of the motion picture. He and his young assistant, William Dickson, met with the two men, and the latter shortly thereafter perfected the first movie machine, the Kinetoscope. This was shown interested visitors in 1891 and was put on the market three years later.

In that year, 1894, Japan also first saw it. Actually, however, Japan's first encounter with the movies had been twenty years earlier when a French astronomer named Janssen had brought an early invention of Marey, a photo-gun called a *fusil photographique,* into the country. The event was not publicized because Janssen took pictures only straight up. He had come to this sometimes foggy and often rainy country in order to photograph the transit of Venus. This accomplished, he returned, and Japan's first encounter with the cinema passed uncelebrated.

Not the second. A Kobe gentleman named Shinji Takahashi lugged one of the Dickson-Edison peep-show machines into the hotel bedroom of His Imperial Highness, Prince Komatsu, where the royal personage proclaimed himself "delighted with the demonstration," and the newspapers next day were full of the pleasing combination of royal Japanese condescension and Western inventive know-how.

First the Prince and then all Japan saw the boxing matches and variety-turns which made up the peep-show program. The problem remained that only one person could see at a time, but the machines were quite popular, and indeed still are, with the difference that it is now nude ladies rather than boxers which inspire attention.

The built-in restriction of the Kinetoscope was, in the meantime, being studied abroad. In England, William Friese-Greene, experimenting with projection, had by 1890 managed to capture a degree of movement at Hyde Park corner. In the same year F. H. Varley had made a real motion-picture camera, using the idea of sprocket holes in film which earlier, in 1888, had been patented (without avail, it would seem) by Louis-Augustin Le Prince. Edison, always the businessman, approached his neighbor, George Eastman; Dickson got perforated celluloid strips to work with, and the film industry was born.

Its birth was accompanied by the chaos of duplication, competition, and waste which customarily characterizes infant industries. Two English engineers, Birt Acres and William Paul, had between them managed to make a machine which enabled a showing of the 1896 derby on the evening of the day it was run. In France, the Lumiére brothers, making use of the inventions of Emile Reynaud, had constructed their *cinématographe*. Finally, Thomas Armat had perfected a machine called a Vitascope which he unveiled in Atlanta in 1895. For box-office reasons his name was coupled with that of Edison and the premiere caused a sensation in New York.

It caused a sensation in Japan as well, the Vitascope being introduced in Osaka in 1897. The first mixed bill showed flood scenes and a collision at sea, a choice peculiarly apt in that these initial three-day performances constituted a benefit for the victims of the sunken Japanese vessel, "Sanko Maru." A month later, the Vitascope moved into a regular theater where the stellar attraction was a Miss Fuller doing the "butterfly dance" in what passed for the semi-nude.

Vitascope had competition in Japan as elsewhere. Just a week before its grand opening, a man named Katsutaro Inahata had begun showings using the Lumiére machine. Among the fifty films he brought back from France were shots of the arrival of a train at the Gare du Nord, and views of Deauville. These last were particularly enjoyed, the spectators ducking lest they get wet. Also in attendance was a young gentleman from Lyon, a M. Durel, who came with the machine and is locally remembered for gadding about exotic Osaka and for finally bungling the taking of the first films to be made in Japan.

Vitascope had the lead, however, for it had royalty. The Crown Prince, later the Emperor Taisho, graced a performance and enjoyed the opportunity to view another crowned head, that of the Czar of Russia, though it is reported that he confused him with his coachman, since the one up on the roof was obviously in the superior position. Royal example having been set, the Japanese began crowding into the Vitascope performances in Tokyo. These were shown in a real theater and the prices were just as high as real theater prices.

Japanese audiences obviously felt differently about films from those elsewhere. In America, for example, the early film audiences were found among the less wealthy, and the later "famous plays with famous players" were plainly a lure to respectable (and proportionately more) money. In France, early films were associated with disastrous charity-bazaar film showings during which the *cinématographe* caught fire and killed numbers. The *films d'art* which followed were (at slightly higher prices) an invitation to safe respectability.

In Japan, however, from the first, the movies were completely respectable. They were plainly upper-class entertainment, and this was known because it cost quite a bit to get in to see them. This was to have a definite effect upon Japanese cinema once it got started. In the West, John C. Rice kissing May

Irwin, and Fred Ott sneezing, appealed strongly only to the groundlings. Later on, such grateful subjects as train robberies, the lives of firemen, and being rescued by Rover were equally welcomed. This was low fare indeed to respectable Edwardian audiences, and movies were thought no more genteel than the boxing matches they had originally immortalized. It is in the nature of the motion picture, however, that just such subjects are best, because the main thing about movies is that they move. In the West, from the first, there were sneezes, bandits, and firemen racing to the rescue; it is to such subjects that the motion picture is peculiarly suited, discomfiting though this proved to the genteel.

In Japan, however, the audience was in itself extremely genteel, and so therefore was early Japanese cinema. The Japanese had their "famous plays with famous players" long before the idea occurred to Adolph Zukor or Charles Pathé. Mr. Inahata and M. Durel having somehow ruined the footage of things Japanese requested by the Lumiére brothers, the first films taken in Japan were made by Tsunekichi Shibata of the Mitsukoshi Department Store's newly-formed photographic department. These included shots taken on the Ginza, views of the more respectable geisha, and the kabuki.

Originally, the Vitascope opening was to have occurred at the Kabuki-za, home of the traditional Japanese theater. The leading actor of the day, Danjuro IX, put his foot down. He was against foreign innovations on principle, and one glimpse of the Dickson-Edison boxing matches convinced him that the precincts of the Kabuki-za would provide no home for such evidence of Western and barbaric ways.

Having refused the projector, the famous actor somewhat surprisingly accepted the camera. Shibata prevailed upon him to have his picture taken. He and Kikugoro V graciously allowed the filming of a small section of the kabuki version of the noh drama, *Maple Viewing*, and this occurred outdoors in back of the Kabuki-za at the end of 1899. There was one showing, a private one, in the summer of 1900, at Danjuro's home, and he professed himself delighted with it, though he had earlier extracted the promise that it would not be shown publicly during his lifetime, preferring to think of the alm as a purely commemorative gesture.

The next year, however, he suddenly fell ill when scheduled to appear in Osaka. Kikugoro was already dead, and Danjuro himself did not expect to last much longer; he permitted the film to be shown so that the audience would not be disappointed. The film was to have been shown a week. When Danjuro died, four months later, it was still playing.

The movies had arrived, but they had arrived in Japan with a difference. They were an expensive entertainment, graced by royalty, patronized by the leaders of society, and condescended to (albeit unwillingly) by the leading kabuki actors of the day. From the first there was a confusion with the theater, an ill which the nascent cinema in other countries encountered only later, when it was better able to cope. Since the cinema was thought an adjunct of the stage, early film showings in Japan carried most of the trappings of the Japanese theater. This included banging drums at the beginning of each performance, and the constant attendance of the *benshi*, that lecture-commentator whose ancestors have a definite place in *bunraku* (Japan's puppet theater) and kabuki, but whose cinematic services were usually restricted to commenting upon the apparent and explaining the obvious. With such constant availability of spoken commentary, it was not necessary for the infant Japanese cinema to invent continuity. Thus, while a necessary film grammar was already being evolved by England's Frank Mottershaw in the 1903 *A Daylight Burglary* and by Edwin S. Porter in *The Great Train Robbery* of the same year, the Japanese pictures remained someone talking through moving lantern-slides. Explanations, then as now, were enormously popular in Japan, where an informed audience is a happy one. The *benshi* were both beloved and rewarded. In the advertisements of the period, their names were often larger than the titles of those films they were ostensibly accompanying.

The confusion of stage and screen is seen in other ways. One of the early films, the 1899 *Scene of the Lightning Robber's Being Arrested*, was made as an advertisement for the stage show. Shown along with *Mary, Queen of Scots*, or *Les quatre têtes embarrassantes*, it invited the audience to step next door after their present entertainment was concluded. Around 1904, when the *rensa-geki*, or "chain-drama," was evolved, both stage and screen got together in the same theater at the same time. The most popular of these interesting hybrids was *Otomi Stabbed*, a 1908 creation in which filmed scenes on the screen alternated with live-action scenes on the stage, a technique somewhat similar to that used later for *Entr'acte* and *Lulu*, a resemblance ending there in that the *rensa-geki* did not presume the sophistication of Satie or Berg.

A parallel is seen in the 1908 French *film d'art* called *l'Assassinat du Duc de Guise*, a piece of theater enacted by members of the Comédie Française, accompanied by an especially written score from the pen of Camille Saint-Saëns. It is said that the producer, Charles Pathé, approached Le Bargy, the principal actor, after the performances and, with brimming eyes, said: "Oh, you gentlemen are indeed our masters!"—a remark considered so uncinematic that it is recorded in film histories. In Japan both tears and speech would have been thought apt, because here the stage was in actuality the stern mistress that she is often said to be. Movies were to be just like the stage.

With one important exception. In Japan, theater is actors' theater—the audience goes to see so-and-so in such-and-such, and not the other way around. The movies could boast only the provincial and the second-rate. Even with the great Danjuro's example, no well-known actor would have appeared before the camera, even though the Kabuki-za itself showed films. What was needed was a star, some actor to go see *in* a film, someone to talk about, someone to sigh over and feel for. The films had the *benshi*, to be sure, but a more complete empathy was needed. This lack was remedied with the discovery of Matsunosuke Onoe.

Maple Viewing, 1898. A scene from the kabuki with Kikugoro Onoe V and Danjuro Ichikawa IX.

Matsunosuke Onoe in the title-role of the movie *Jiraiya*.

MATSUNOSUKE ONOE was almost thirty when Shozo Makino discovered him playing in a provincial kabuki troupe. Makino owned a theater and occasionally made one-reelers for the local companies. By this time there were more than a few. The Konishi Camera Company had filmed scenes of Ginza geisha as well as the lightning-robber getting caught; Tsunekichi Doi had gone to America to construct the teahouse for the Chicago Exposition and stayed on to study with Edison, returning to photograph *sumo* (Japanese wrestling) and show the results with a phonograph recording of crowd-noises, thus creating the first "talkie"; and Kenichi Kawaura, owner of the company that had imported the *cinématographe* and who went to the Edison and Lubin studios, returned in 1908, built himself a villa in imitation of Méliès and a studio in imitation of Edison. It was he who shortly became president of the first major Japanese company, and it was here that Makino brought Matsunosuke. The actor caught on at once with the audience. It was not that his skill was so extreme; it was that the timing of his appearance was so precise. The movies were a business, and the native audience needed a native star. His popularity became so great that between 1909 and 1911 he and Makino made almost 170 films together, including the popular *Jiraiya*, and the first film version of the kabuki, *Sukeroku*.

13

Members of the Matsunosuke Onoe group. Left to right: Sentaro Nakamura, Enichiro Jitsukawa, and Chosei Kataoka.

FOR TEN years, Matsunosuke was the only actor who could be called a star in the modern sense of the word. During the height of his popularity he turned out eight features a month and was sometimes under orders to make a reel a day. This was not so difficult as it now sounds. The director usually read the *benshi* dialogue aloud and the actors made up their own business. So long as they stayed within the indicated sight lines they were quite visible, since camera position was never changed. When a roll of film ended, they were warned not to move, and the camera was reloaded—a process which was known to take up to half an hour. In making these pictures Makino was quite content to present scenes for the *benshi* to talk through, and his sole innovation was to adapt the "pace" of American pictures. This had impressed him, but it is typical of these early days that instead of having Matsunosuke act faster, he shot the film at eight frames per second rather than the usual sixteen. The resultant scurrying about impressed everyone with its modernity.

14

MATSUNOSUKE gathered about him a number of minor kabuki actors, among them Sentaro Nakamura, Enichiro Jitsukawa, and Chosei Kataoka, and together they made a great number of films, of which *Sukeroku* is an example. This filming of a popular kabuki featuring a "star" shares much with Sarah Bernhardt's *Queen Elizabeth*—just as Louis Mercanton shares much with Shozo Makino. Both attempted some compromise with the new medium— less expansive gestures, some psychological interpretation; both films were very talky, though both are silent; both are shot from the single viewpoint of the spectator at a play; both had subjects all but hallowed by popular approval; both were as unsuited to film as they were suited to the stage; and both were extremely popular. For some early showings Mercanton even used a *compère*, the French equivalent of the *benshi*.

Scenes from a film version of the kabuki, *Sukeroku*.

 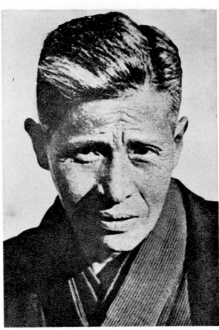

LEFT: a scene from Shozo Makino's film version of the kabuki, *The Loyal Forty-seven Ronin*, with Anezo Ichikawa (left) and Matsunosuke Onoe. RIGHT: Shozo Makino.

THE *compère* faded rapidly away. The *benshi* did not. He continued to exercise his influence into the sound era. The restrictions he imposed were considerable. The innovations of D. W. Griffith and Thomas Ince were called into being because, other than the use of titles, there was no way to portray character except through action. The movement-filled plots, the close-up, the flashback—all were invented to answer this need for character explication. In Japan there was no such need because the *benshi* were always there with full explanations. The 1913 Makino version of *The Loyal Forty-seven Ronin*—both a kabuki and a film perennial—is an example. The cuts are enormously long (the full amount of film that could be loaded for one take into the early cameras); the camera position never shifts, nor does the camera pan. Matsunosuke emotes and, during the high points, plays directly into the lens. The charm of this and other of the early films is considerable but it remains that. We are not involved, as we are in re-seeing Griffith films of the same period. Both Matsunosuke and Makino were so innocent of intentions other than that of recreating a stage play that we find the picture charming, as we find old newsreels charming. To see *The New York Hat*, however, made in the same year, is to worry about Mary Pickford, to feel for her dashed hopes, and to jubilate when the kindly clergyman intervenes. Japan was at least ten years behind the cinematic times.

TEN YEARS behind the cinematic times—which is not too surprising. Japan was not yet half a century away from the "splendid isolation" which insisted upon both land tenure and hara-kiri. A mature Japanese seeing Matsunosuke might well have remembered himself wearing the double swords of the samurai. In fact, the continuing popularity of the period film (and Japan makes more costume pictures than any other country) might be that the period, after all, is not so far distant. Further, during the rapidly changing and unsettling days of the Meiji period, such reminders of a securely feudal Tokugawa era were comforting. This was perhaps one of the reasons behind the Japanese willingness to confuse stage and screen. The stage (at least the kabuki and the *bunraku*) is a traditional theater in that it continues its

16

traditionally feudal ways; its virtues are all those of the Tokugawa period. A real problem faced the film in Japan because it is not a medium well suited to historical reconstruction. The motion-picture camera is able to capture the precise look of things, and if the things are reconstructed then they look precisely reconstructed. In addition, this "realism" which is the major attribute of the camera did not suit the Japanese eye, which (strong as it is in other qualities) has never been attentive to the "realistic" aspects of whatever it looks at. Ruskin was being very cinematic when he enthused over the "sensational realism" of motion-picture views of Venice, because it is just this appearance of reality which film is capable of capturing, but his views would have cut little ice in Japan, where surface is usually dismissed as superficial, and reality is not real until it has been arranged. The forest is made into a park which looks like a forest; the landscape-garden is a garden which is like a landscape; and flower-arranging insists upon flowers purposefully arranged. Things as they are, things as you find them, things accidental and fortuitous have never been popular in Japan. In fact, the symbol of the country might be the *bonsai*, a fully grown tree which is one foot high. In this country where nature is forced to imitate art, it would follow that films would be categorized with what was recognized as the most closely allied Japanese art—the stage. Not that the influence of the kabuki was regarded as entirely beneficial. Still, it is typical that in an attempt to properly place the film it was not separated from drama but was early allied with, instead, merely a later form of drama, the *shimpa*. This genre had been evolved to offset the feudal extremes of the kabuki, though it shortly incorporated them, and so, after a number of filmed *shimpa*, movies (being modern and Western) were thought to be a department of *shingeki*, the "new theater" which had been evolved shortly before this. If kabuki is Dryden, then *shimpa* is Pinero, and *shingeki* is Eugene O'Neill. The new theater, deriving from Belasco and Western uses of the proscenium-stage, was to be completely realistic, the Japanese having caught up with that trend of thought common in nineteenth-century Europe and America that realism for its own sake was somehow better, an argument in general reminiscent of that which insists that to be poor is to be virtuous. Though Matsunosuke declined, the new "realistic" films were all based on stage-plays. Among the earliest and most popular was the 1914 *Katusha*, made after a *shingeki* adaptation of Tolstoy's *Resurrection*. Directed by Kiyomatsu Hosoyama, a pupil of Makino, it went in heavily for Russian costumes and settings, though it also retained the female impersonator, relic of the kabuki and the *shimpa*.

Katusha, 1914, directed by Kiyomatsu Hosoya, with Sadajiro Tachibana (left) and Tappatsu Sekino.

17

The Living Corpse, 1917, directed by Eizo Tanaka, with Kaichi Yamamoto (left) and Teinosuke Kinugasa.

ANOTHER of the "new" films was Eizo Tanaka's *The Living Corpse* (another Tolstoy adaptation), made in 1917. Though it retained the impersonators (the heroine was Teinosuke Kinugasa, later director of *Crossroads* and *Gate of Hell*), it incorporated such novel techniques as the close-up. The novelty, however, was not extreme because of the way the Japanese used it. When Griffith used his first close-up, in the 1908 *After Many Years*, he did so (as the following images indicated) to show what his heroine was thinking. Tanaka at least—in this picture—did no such thing. The stage-front position of the viewer was maintained, and the close-up meant that the spectator had merely moved to a better seat. Close-ups as indicative of states of mind were not seen until much later. That the close-up was used at all, however, meant an acceptance on the part of the theater-oriented audience. Its introduction was mainly the work of Norimasu Kaeriyama, himself a director and a resolutely anti-*benshi* one at that. He believed that movies could tell their own stories in their own way, and this belief was also held by a number of resourceful movie-makers who had gone abroad to study methods of film-making much as their fathers had gone abroad during the Meiji period to learn how to make ships or construct constitutional law. Among these were Yutaka Abe, Frank Tokunaga, Henry Kotani, and Thomas Kurihara—their names alone indicating a certain amount of foreign travel. The latter,

LEFT: Two views of the Nikkatsu Studios during this period. BELOW: *The Cuckoo*, 1918, directed by Eizo Tanaka, with Hideo Fujino (left) and Takeo Azuma.

having played villains in various Sessue Hayakawa and William S. Hart films, had learned of the importance of the director in American pictures. When he returned, Kurihara brought back not only new production ideas but the extremely original thought that the director should really direct. Given the prestige then as now conferred upon anyone who leaves a small country and then comes back to it, he was given the freedom to make *Amateur Club*, a comedy about a group of amateur kabuki actors at the seaside. It impressed his audience as being too American and too happy. The movies were a serious matter for the Japanese audience. It had paid its money and it demanded a moving experience, preferably tragic since that was somehow more meaningful. In *The Lasciviousness of the Viper*, he brought Kaeriyama's ideas and American know-how to a historical theme (the same which was later the basis of Mizoguchi's *Ugetsu*) and this much more impressed the audience since it was very unhappy indeed. Henry Kotani, who had studied with "Papa" Wycoff, the "father of cameramen," made *Island Woman*, a realistic tragedy starring the kabuki actor, Tsuruzo Nakamura. It was very successful—kabuki wedded to the modern drama through a real star—so much so that for a time Kotani received seven hundred dollars a month, a wage then higher than that of the Premier of Japan.

19

TOP LEFT: *A Woman Standing in the Light*, 1920, directed by Minoru Murata, with Shin Nezu (left) and Kitty Slarabina. RIGHT: *Amateur Club*, 1920, directed by Thomas Kurihara, with Sango Kamiya (left foreground). CENTER LEFT: *Island Woman*, 1920, directed by Henry Kotani, with Yoshiko Kawada (left) and Tsuruzo Nakamura. RIGHT: Henry Kotani.

NEW METHODS are usually accepted by the audience before they are by the head office. Companies were first talked into making movie-like movies by being told that these were only for export. One such film was *A Woman Standing in the Light,* directed by Minoru Murata for Kaoru Osanai. Actually it, and many others, never saw a foreign screen, nor were they intended to. Osanai knew his Japanese businessmen: If he announced that the product was for foreigners he could be as advanced as he pleased because then as now the businessman (to his great disadvantage) remains basically uninterested in anything happening outside his shores. The enterprising camera or transistor manufacturer with foreign branches and booths at trade fairs is an exceptional phenomenon. Much more typical is the standard Japanese movie company which does not answer its foreign mail and turns deaf ears on foreign pleas for films. In this case, however, the indifference of the head office allowed Osanai and others to do just what they wanted, and the stunted infant cinema finally began to take a few steps on its own.

AMONG THE innovations being introduced were a more naturalistic handling of the actors and a more relaxed handling of the camera. An example was *The Mountains Grow Dark*. Though the story smelled of *shimpa*, the direction exuded mainly the fresh fragrance of ideas. There was a concern for character and for detail which was new to Japanese cinema. One of the innovations was that women began to appear in front of the camera. In *Winter Camellia*, Masao Inoue used the young Yaeko Mizutani, who is still one of Japan's finest actresses.

LEFT: *The Mountains Grow Dark*, 1921, directed by Kiyohiko Ushihara, with (from left) Haruko Sawamura, Komei Minami, and Akio Isono. (extreme right) BOTTOM LEFT: *The Lasciviousness of the Viper*, 1921, directed by Thomas Kurihara, with (from left) Tokihiko Okada and Yoko Benizawa. RIGHT: *Winter Camellia*, 1921, directed by Masao Inoue (left) and Yaeko Mizutani.

21

TOP: *The Women and the Pirates*, 1922, directed by Hotei Nomura, with Yoko Umemura and Yotaro Katsumi. CENTER, LEFT TO RIGHT: Yoko Umemura and Sakuko Yanagi; Umeko Sakuragi; Shizuko Mori. BOTTOM: Emiko Yakumo; and Tomoko Makino.

22

ONE OF THE results of the novelty of seeing real women on the screen was that they all became stars. Empathizing with Matsunosuke had become such a national pastime that the opportunity to like someone different—and prettier—was grasped. Souvenir pictures of these girls were sold everywhere, and those of the once-popular geisha and impersonators became less and less in evidence. The most popular of the new stars was Sumiko Kurishima. On one single day in 1922, four thousand copies of her photo were sold in Tokyo alone. To be sure, most of the new heroines were put into films the caliber of *The Women and the Pirates*, but even here is seen evolving a completely feminine style of acting—later to become one of the most attractive aspects of Japanese cinema. Kinuyo Tanaka, for example, still a very active actress, revealed in even her worst early films a grasp of film-acting and its demands of which at least a number of the foreign film actresses were entirely innocent.

ABOVE, LEFT TO RIGHT: Chieko Matsui; Kinuyo Tanaka; Sumiko Kurishima. BOTTOM: Tanaka and Kurishima.

ABOVE: Haruko Sawamura. RIGHT:
Souls on the Road, 1921, directed by
Minoru Murata, with (from left)
Mikio Hisamatsu, Denmei Suzuki,
and Haruko Sawamura.

ANOTHER of the favorites of the day was Haruko Sawamura, who is now
remembered partially because she was in the first really important Japanese
film. This was *Souls on the Road*, a movie which is to Japan as *The Birth of a
Nation* is to America, as *La roue* is to France. Directed by Minoru Murata
and produced by Kaoru Osanai, it consists of two cross-cut stories. One is
about the prodigal who returns penniless, but with wife and child. The other,
taken in part from Gorky's *The Lower Depths*, is about two convicts who
wander the countryside looking for a place to live. These stories, only slightly
connected in theme, are united in *mood*, in atmosphere, a quality very strong
in this film, and later to become one of the strengths of the Japanese cinema.
The reason, in part, for the atmosphere was that *Souls on the Road* was one
of the first Japanese films to be made almost entirely away from the studio.
It was actually filmed in the fields and along the roads. The scenes look real
because they *are* real: the black fields of late winter, the dead grasses, the
gray skies of early spring, the dark roads leading endlessly across the land.
This was also among the first Japanese pictures to provide a constant background which both sustained the action and commented upon it. Later,
Cavalcanti in *En rade*, Karl Grune in *Die Strasse*, and many more including
Fellini in *La Strada*, were to use the street or the roads as a place where
the apparently fortuitous—so necessary, so grateful to the eye of the camera
—can occur. There can be no plot if the fortuitous is allowed, and it was

24

LEFT: Minoru Murata. RIGHT: *Souls on the Road*, with Komei Minami (left) and Takeo Tsunami.

perhaps for this reason that Murata preferred using episodes—and even these are "open-ended" because, having no plot, the film can have no conclusion. The prodigal and his wife and child wander; the two convicts wander; and the result is a kind of immediacy which plot cannot contrive nor studio manufacture. The film made a great impression upon its audience. The Japanese audience is usually receptive to mood—some of the more admired woodcut prints are nothing *but* mood—and is always impressed by tragedy; and wandering homeless in this land where the well-knit family is the only security is indeed tragic. The audience was also impressed that the people in *Souls on the Road* were neither ladies nor pirates but were completely ordinary people from the lower middle classes. Due to the mildly aristocratic and fashionable beginnings of cinema in Japan, few indeed had been the appearances of the poor, unless they could be shown as picturesque fishing-folk or the like. One of the tenets of realism, however, is that the poor are more real than the rich (and *The Lower Depths* at one time threatened to become the most performed of all *shingeki* drama), so it was perfectly appropriate that through the stage door, as it were, the common folk entered cinema. In this film, ordinary people were indeed shown with a realism and an honesty which, even now, are impressive. In this respect, the picture remains quite the equal of the Griffith or the Gance.

LEFT, TOP TO BOTTOM: *The Kyoya Collar Shop*, 1922, directed by Eizo Tanaka, with (from left) Takeo Azuma, Kenichi Miyajima, Hideo Fujino, and Kasuke Koizumi. *The Quiet Two*, 1922, directed by Gengo Obora, with Utako Nakayama (left). *Razor*, 1923, directed by Yasujiro Shimazu, with Saburo Kojima (left), Chiyoko Mimura and Sakuko Yanagi (middle), and Nobuko Satsuki (right). *A Story of the Streets*, 1924, directed by Kiyomatsu Hosoyama, with Shizuko Mori (right). RIGHT CENTER: *Love of Life*, 1923, directed by Kiyohiko Ushihara, with Chiyoko Mimura (left), Yukichi Iwata and Yoko Umemura (right). BOTTOM: *Seisaku's Wife*, 1924, directed by Minoru Murata, with Koichi Katsuragi.

26

TOP LEFT: *Hanpeita Tsukigata*, 1925, directed by Teinosuke Kinugasa, with Shojiro Sawada. RIGHT: *The Song of the Boatman*, 1923, directed by Gishun Ikeda, with Yukichi Iwata (left) and Sumiko Kurishima. CENTER LEFT: *Collar Button*, 1926, directed by Hotei Nomura, with Tsuzuya Moroguchi (left) and Yukiko Tsukuba. RIGHT: *Father*, 1924, directed by Yasujiro Shimazu, with Hiroshi Masakuni (left) and Yaeko Mizutani.

ONE OF THE results of the acceptance of *Souls on the Road* was that, for the first time in Japan, directors were free to make films about Japanese life as it was. This had already occurred abroad where the influence of the *film d'art* was soon cast aside. *Assunta Spina* was about a working-class girl; Epstein's *Le coeur fidèle* was about real—if criminal—middle-class folk. Among these later new films in Japan (a genre which came to be known as *shomin-geki* and was to have decisive importance in the shaping of a national cinema) were: Eizo Tanaka's *The Kyoya Collar Shop*, a tragedy laid in a small-business setting; *The Quiet Two*, a drama about a middle-class mother and her child; Gishin Ikeda's *The Song of the Boatman*, a domestic tragedy starring Sumiko Kurishima; Kiyomatsu Hosoyama's *A Story of the Streets*; Kiyohiko Ushihara's *Love of Life*; Teinosuke Kinugasa's *Hanpeita Tsukigata*; Murata's *Seisaku's Wife*, the tragedy of a man and wife parted by the social prejudices occasioned by her having been a prostitute, and a number by Yasujiro Shimizu. These included *Razor*, a six-reel social-drama, and *Father*, one of the first of the *shomin-geki* comedies, a film about a baseball champion and a country girl which seemed to suggest that middle-class life need not be entirely dark. This kind of common-sense comedy, to be seen later in films of Gosho, Naruse, Ozu, and Toyoda, was very attractive in Hotei Nomura's *Collar Button*, and in several films by a new director, Kenji Mizoguchi. One of his middle-class comedies was *Turkeys in a Row*, a film which starred the young Hiroshi Inagaki, later to become famous as the director of the Academy-Award-winning *Samurai*.

LEFT: *Turkeys in a Row*, 1924, directed by Kenji Mizoguchi, with Kasuke Koizumi (left) and Hiroshi Inagaki. BELOW: *A Paper Doll's Whisper of Spring*, 1926, directed by Kenji Mizoguchi, with Tokihiko Okada (left) and Yoko Umemura.

KENJI MIZOGUCHI, along with Murata and Shimazu one of the finest of the new directors, went on to become world famous with *Ugetsu*. Born in 1898, he was trained as an artist, and this background was partially responsible for his having created some of the most pictorially beautiful of all Japanese films. At the same time, he had a very real interest in the *shomin-geki*, a form which he did much to develop, and with a photographic realism that insisted things be shown as they are. To do this is to criticize, and to criticize is to meet opposition. It is very fortunate that Mizoguchi possessed in large measure what Akira Kurosawa has called "his amazing push," because no sooner had he convinced his producers that it was all right to show the joys and sorrows of ordinary people, than he demanded that they finance films which showed the injustice upon which the sorrows were based. One of these was *A Paper Doll's Whisper of Spring*, a film about a love affair doomed by poverty, which stated flatly that it is hard to be happy without money, a social truth which was—to the producers at least—most unwelcome.

28

ANOTHER DIRECTOR later to become much better known was Teinosuke Kinugasa. One of the films which brought about his fame was *A Page Out of Order*, about a sailor who has been the cause of his wife's insanity and takes a job in the asylum where she is kept. The interesting thing about this picture is not only that it honestly depicts a rather unpleasant subject, but that it created a subjective view of the hero's world rather in the manner of *Das Kabinett des Doctor Caligari*, a film which had not at that time yet been seen in Japan. This is the ideal (indeed the only) way to present acute suffering, which is probably one of the reasons that the Kinugasa and the Weine films seem to resemble each other. Another, however, is that neither director had enough money to do what he wanted. The German, in order to save electricity, painted shadows on the *Caligari* sets; the Japanese, who didn't have enough lights, painted his studio set with silver paint, which accounts for the unearthly luminosity of some of his images. Just as Paul Leni in *Das Wachsfigurenkabinett* was forced to suggest rather than to show, particularly in the fine Jack-the-Ripper sequence, completed after the funds were used up, so Kinugasa, with not enough money, not enough people, was forced to invent ways (use of shadows, odd camera angles selected so that the tinyness of the set would not be exposed) and turn his poverty into an asset. The approach distinguished the film, and the audience liked it—fortunately for Kinugasa, or else his film-making days would have been over: he had gone heavily into debt to complete the picture.

BELOW LEFT: *A Page Out of Order*, 1927, directed by Teinosuke Kinugasa, with Masao Inoue. RIGHT: scene during the filming. BOTTOM: *The Woman Who Touched the Legs*, 1926, directed by Yutaka Abe, with Tokihiko Okada (left) and Yoko Umemura.

A PAGE OUT OF ORDER was made in 1927; *Caligari* was made ten years earlier in 1918. Though the two films are not otherwise closely comparable, they both have an independence of thought which took at least ten years longer to evolve in Japan than it did in Europe. That a picture such as Kinugasa's could now be popularly accepted was an indication that times had changed. By the end of the 1920's the feudal era was something read about in history books, and those who could personally remember the days of the top-knot and the double swords were all well over sixty. Even the Meiji era was regarded with that impatient tolerance which the West reserved for the Victorian. Now, it was said, times were different. All of the men (though none of the women) could vote, liberal statesmen could say what they thought, and there was a new emperor whose reign, Showa, means "enlightened peace." Though both army and navy had already embarked on that disastrous course which would all but destroy their country, both government and emperor remained relatively unaware; the people, of course, knew nothing at all. Rather, it seemed that a new age was dawning, an age of true enlightenment, even of democracy. This was one of the reasons that the *shomin-geki* took such hold of the imagination of the period. For the first time it was openly realized that the fish-monger down the street was little different (except financially) from the mogul on the hill, and this realization made for a new feeling of freedom for both monger and mogul alike. Even women, traditionally underprivileged, felt the breath of freedom. Girls smoked in public, the flapper became the rage, and the exceptionally daring even held hands with their boyfriends while enjoying a fashionable stroll along the Ginza. Young men almost indiscriminately interested themselves in the principles of constitutional law, the novels of Zola, the theories of Karl Marx, and the science of knife and fork. This period was the first—

TOP LEFT: *A Tricky Girl*, 1927, directed by Heinosuke Gosho, with Emiko Yakumo (left) and Atsushi Watanabe. RIGHT: *A Diary of Chuji's Travel*, 1927, directed by Daisuke Ito, with Denjiro Okochi. CENTER LEFT: *The Wandering Gambler*, 1928, directed by Hiroshi Inagaki, with Chiezo Kataoka. RIGHT: *The Brilliant Showa Period*, 1928, directed by Yasujiro Shimazu, with Masao Inoue (left) and Shoichi Fujido.

30

and the last until after the Second World War—where the man on the street began to feel like a real individual with definite and personal ideas. Having become interested in himself, he could afford to become interested in others. Thus, he liked the new cinema which was about real people in real situations.

Particularly popular were films which had social messages, or films which viewed history from a new angle. Yutaka Abe's oddly-titled *The Woman Who Touched the Legs* showed the new woman tolerating no nonsense from the traditional Japanese male; Gosho's *A Tricky Girl* was an affectionate farce-comedy-melodrama about the poor—Eisenstein saw it and said it began like a Monty Banks comedy and ended in deepest despair; Shimazu's *The Brilliant Showa Period* was a sarcastic comedy about feudal remnants during this new era of "enlightened peace." In *A Diary of Chuji's Travels*, Daisuke Ito showed that the feudal hero had democratic principles at heart; Hiroshi Inagaki's *A Swordsman's Picture Book* and *The Wandering Gambler* showed the Tokugawa period as it probably was, shorn of all romance. Among the other new directors who supplied for the new demand were Tomu Uchida with *Cannon Smoke and a Rain of Shells*, Hiroshi Shimizu with *A Happy Song*, and Shiro Toyoda with his debut film, *Painted Lips*. All of these pictures (along with many others, including those of Kiyohiko Ushihara, and in particular, *The Great City*) shared the single assumption that Japanese films should be about Japanese life and should show it as fully and as honestly as possible. This is a revolutionary belief and one which, in any country, usually runs into producer trouble. One of the reasons that in Japan it was both allowed and gratified was that the Japanese public liked this reflection of itself. Here were real people, real individuals, and this is just what the movie-goer had recently discovered that he himself was.

CENTER LEFT: *Cannon Smoke and a Rain of Shells*, 1928, directed by Tomu Uchida, with Eiji Nakano. RIGHT: *A Happy Song*, 1929, directed by Hiroshi Shimizu, with Atsushi Watanabe (left) and Kinuyo Tanaka. BOTTOM LEFT: *A Swordsman's Picture Book*, 1929, directed by Hiroshi Inagaki, with Nobuko Fushimi (left) and Chiezo Kataoka. RIGHT: *Painted Lips*, 1929, directed by Shiro Toyoda, with Shizue Takita (left) and Shinyo Nara.

LEFT, TOP TO BOTTOM: *The Great City*, 1929, directed by Kiyohiko Ushihara, with Denmei Suzuki (left) and Kinuyo Tanaka; Denmei Suzuki on location for *The Dusty World*, 1924; director Kenji Mizoguchi seen between the cameras; Nobuo Asaoka (right) with Mitsuyo Hara in the *Wolf of the Rails*, 1927. CENTER: Tsunemi Hirose in Tomu Uchida's *The Sea-loving Son Sails Away*, 1929. BOTTOM Momonosuke Ichikawa in Minoru Ishiyama's 1918 *Nagatonokami Kimura*.

LEFT TO RIGHT: Chiezo Kataoka; Denjiro Okochi; Ryunosuke Tsukigata. Tsumasaburo Bando in the *Darkness*, 1928; Chojiro Hayashi (Kazuo Hasegawa) in the *Blizzard Pass*, 1929.

ANOTHER reason for the willingness of the audience is that new times need new heroes, and supplying them is one of the major concerns of any motion-picture industry. The Japanese public, however, is different from that in other countries in that it likes to be shown to itself as it is, not as it might be. The familiar is considered reassuring, more so in Japan than anywhere else, and much of the honesty of the Japanese films—that it is, indeed, a real reflection of the country—is because this audience likes best what it already knows. The idols in America during this period were Corinne Griffith in ermine or Bebe Daniels in egret feathers; in Japan it was Akiko Chihaya weeping or Kinuyo Tanaka making like a flapper. American women did not often see ermine and egret but wanted their favorite film stars smothered in it. Japanese women, on the other hand, weep very often indeed, and like to play the flapper themselves. And that is the difference. The men also differed from their Western cousins. Denmei Suzuki (who early appeared in a minor Mizoguchi film where he fought with a man dressed in a bear suit) became one of the leading screen heroes because he was so much like everyone else; also because, along with an invincible mediocrity, he had ideas of his own. This winning combination, both reassuring and challenging, is possible in films—witness Richard Barthelmess—and made Suzuki one of the most popular male stars of the period. Others of the new heroes included such samurai with modern consciences as Ryunosuke Tsukigata, Tsumazaburo Bando, Chiezo Kataoka, Denjiro Okochi, Momonosuke Ichikawa, and Chojiro Hayashi; the latter, whose name is now Kazuo Hasegawa, is still one of the leading actors. More approaching the Hollywood pattern were the equally popular Tsunemi Hirose, an athletic young man who resembled a more restrained William Haines, and Nobuo Asaoka. Since one of the ways to achieve success in Japan is to take something Western and add that little touch which makes it Japanese, Asaoka was extremely popular. Everyone agreed that he looked, possibly talked and certainly *acted* just like Richard Dix.

33

STILL ANOTHER of the new actors was Junosuke Bando, who became fairly well known abroad thanks to a single picture, one of the silent period's finest films. This was Teinosuke Kinugasa's *Crossroads*. In it the director continued the subjective-viewpoint experiments of *A Page Out of Order* and created a film which, when shown abroad as *Shadows of the Yoshiwara*, impressed many European critics—the last Japanese film to do so until *Rashomon*. The two pictures have something in common: both question simple reality and both were accused of being "non-Japanese," whatever that means. In *Crossroads*, a young man thinks he has killed a man. Wounded, he goes to his sister for help; she goes to an official who tries to seduce her and she kills him. The young man then discovers that the man he thought he had killed is alive. Weak from loss of blood, he dies from the shock. The story is an unexpected one—even in 1928 heroic samurai were expected to be heroic, not to run off to female siblings for assistance and then die from the shock of *not* having killed someone. Equally unexpected was Kinugasa's method of presenting the story. Since the distraught hero is no longer able to distinguish past from present, the film has no use for chronology and so dispenses with it. Also, the emotions of the hero are presented in such a way that the audience must share them. The sister is seen, not in her room, but against the childhood memories her brother now recalls; the pain becomes a visible hallucination when the water he is drinking turns into steam; the most ordinary of objects are transformed—the cat, for example, turns into a great and mythic beast, attracted by the bloom of his open wounds. Kinugasa's use of objects (the cat, the umbrella, the cup, etc.) was and still is fairly rare in Japanese film. Louis Delluc thought that objects were, or could be, as important as people and showed it in his pictures. But the close-up of the hand, the flower, the telephone, pregnant with meaning, were not usual in a Japanese movie. One of the reasons might have been that the Japanese need to see everything in its totality. They need the big picture so that they, as viewers, can be in command of the situation. The use of objects purposely disorients and is designed to disturb, or at least to impress. Even now one rarely sees an object for its own sake on the Japanese screen. It must instead pay its own way. The flower arrangement, if allowed a close-up, must make up for it by becoming a part of later action, though there are many exceptions to this, particularly in the later films of Ozu. In the ordinary Japanese

34

Crossroads, 1928, directed by Teinosuke Kinugasa. Scenes from the film with Junnosuke Bando (male role), Akiko Chihaya and Sumako Uranami.

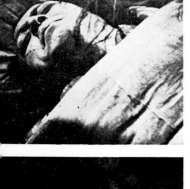

film the close-up of a gun simply means that it is going to go off later. Kinugasa's apparently gratuitous use of cat and wound seemed quite daring to the audience because the cat played no further role in the plot.

Equally impressive was that this picture was one of the first which forced its audience to identify. Not that the problem of simple identification has ever been great in Japan. Ladies at the kabuki always cry at the time-honored and hence proper places. Even now movie advertisements warn if tears are to be expected, and there used to be a grading system, much made fun of now but taken quite seriously before the war, which divided cinema into one-, two- or three-handkerchief films. The problem is with an identification any greater than simple. The reason that such a completely evolving character as a Lear or a Phaedre has never appeared on Japanese stage nor screen is probably that the Japanese are not willing to entertain an empathy any deeper than trival emotionalism and facile tears. *Crossroads*—and a number of pictures to follow—were different in that they demanded more. Much has been made of the "expressionist" quality of both this picture and *A Page Out of Order*, but perhaps the most important result of this seeing from the viewpoint of the hero was that the audience was forced to identify with the hero in a way completely uncommon to Japanese entertainments. Just as in the films of Antonioni, the extraordinary length of some of the shots and the fact that nothing occurs within them makes us search (and find) meaning in the half-smile of Monica Vitti, or the way she looks at her fingernails; so, in this picture, the viewer is forced to reconstruct the story all by himself, coming more and more to feel concern for and with the dying hero. The film was much attacked because, as was rightly pointed out, this was not the Japanese way. The audience responded but somewhat obliquely. The Japanese like puzzles, and the mood of the times was just frivolous enough to make the film the *Marienbad* of its era. Critical comment was stilled (as was to happen again with *Rashomon*) when, after its Berlin showings in 1929, the only film that foreign critics could find to compare it with was Carl Dreyer's newly-released *La Passion de Jeanne d'Arc*. In the meantime, the public had gone on and made the picture a financial success, just as two decades later it was to respond and make the critically-attacked *Rashomon* into one of the most financially successful films of 1950.

THE AUDIENCE determines what kinds of motion pictures are made. This is true whether it shows preference by insisting or by merely accepting what is thrust upon it. Just as the Japanese ability to accept things as they actually are accounts in part for the honesty of Japanese cinema, so the preoccupation of the Japanese with his past largely accounts for the continued popularity of the period-film. In Japan, however, as elsewhere, much of the appeal of the past is that it is, after all, passed, dead. It is summed up, decided upon. We accept the accomplished fact of this or that historical period and are rarely forced to consider that it too was once alive, growing, evolving, problematical to those living within it. Historical films, like historical novels, are always popular, and the reason seems to be that they usually contrast the safely dead past with the possibly dangerous living present. We know what to think about what is gone—a person or an era. We never know what to think about what is here. In most Japanese period films the Tokugawa era becomes a never-never land with impossibly victorious swordsmen and damsels in unlikely, if utter, distress. The appeal is as romantic as *Captain Blood*, on one hand, and *La belle et le bête*, on the other. We live in a present consisting only of "open-ended" stories. Historical entertainments purposely limit this endlessness which is so disconcerting an aspect of living. In a country as enamored of categorizing, of "being sure" as Japan, the appeal of a faithful and certain past is extreme. And so perhaps one of the reasons for the success of *Crossroads* was that it was, after all, a period film. At the same time, the strength of the Kinugasa film lay just in that it forced a deeper empathy and understanding with and for the hero. The result was the ex-

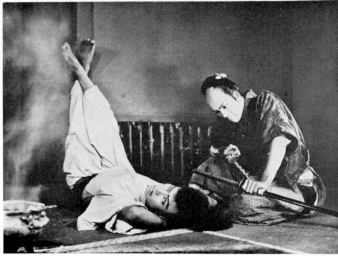

LEFT TO RIGHT: *The Street of Masterless Samurai*, 1928, directed by Masahiro Makino, with Komei Minami; *Ooka's Trial*, 1928, directed by Daisuke Ito, with Denjiro Okochi; *Beheading Place*, 1929, directed by Masahiro Makino, with Seizaburo Kawazu (left) and Juro Tanizaki. *The Rise and Fall of the Shinsengumi*, 1930 directed by Daisuke Ito, with Denjiro Okochi (sitting). *Man-slashing, Horse-piercing Sword*, 1930, directed by Daisuke Ito, with Ryunosuke Tsukigata (left) and Junichi Amano.

hilarating if uneasy feeling that the past is, after all, alive. This idea is not so revolutionary in Japan as elsewhere—in America, for example, where, beginning with *Stagecoach* and continuing through *Red River* and *Shane*, the departures from Tom Mix and Hoot Gibson were considered so extreme that a new term ("adult Western") was found necessary. In Japan the past remains alive in many of the clothes and tools and attitudes of thought, and there is, in addition, a reverence for the past (for old people, for example), which makes the national attitude toward past ages more ambiguous than it is in most countries.

Even before *Crossroads*, there were at least several pictures which suggested that the past be seen as though it were real. Masahiro Makino, son of Shozo, was one of the earliest to work in what became a new genre, the "adult period-film," as it were, in pictures such as *The Street of Masterless Samurai* and *Beheading Place*. One of the first masters of the "living" historical film, a line which was to extend to Mizoguchi's *Ugetsu*, Kurosawa's *Seven Samurai*, and Kobayashi's *Harakiri*, was Daisuke Ito—still active in films—whose best early pictures were *The Rise and Fall of the Shinsengumi*, and the 1930 *Man-Slashing, Horse-Piercing Sword*. These pictures treated Tokugawa society as though it were contemporary: their heroes had the same problems as the man in the balcony. At the same time these, and others, by equating the past with the present in a meaningful and understandable way, very often criticized the present by showing that the past continued to live into the present. A masterless samurai in a Daisuke Ito picture fighting against official corruption could have been anyone in the audience.

THIS NEW spirit of criticism which found its way into the entertainments of the period was a protest not against the new liberality of the government nor against new social ideas; it was against an economy which was felt to be unfair. Neither socialism nor communism was involved (and the police were busy stamping out what timid beginnings they found), but the feeling of need for reform was strong enough. Japan had experienced a serious recession several years earlier and suffered from the international depression of 1930. The protest was therefore against that golden calf with hoofs of clay —capitalism. Pictures such as Gosho's *A New Kind of Woman* and Shimazu's *Revue Sisters* were relatively outspoken in their implications of a corrupt and money-mad upper class; *He and Life* of Kiyohiko Ushihara, though purposely sentimental, remained firmly on the side of the under-privileged. Shigeyoshi Suzuki's *What Made Her Do It?*, based on a popular *shingeki* play, presented a most sympathetic view of a poor girl up against a corrupt and materialistic society. When the film was first shown, it occasioned a riot of enthusiasm, with shouts of "down with capitalism" from the audience. It was also the biggest hit in the history of Japanese silent cinema and ran for months.

38

OPPOSITE PAGE, TOP LEFT: *Nihonbashi*, 1929, directed by Kenji Mizoguchi, with Tokihiko Okada (left) and Yoko Umemura. RIGHT: *He and Life*, 1929, directed by Kiyohiko Ushihara, with Kinuyo Tanaka (left) and Denmei Suzuki. CENTER LEFT: *I Graduated, But...*, 1929, directed by Yasujiro Ozu, with Minoru Takita (left) and Kinuyo Tanaka. RIGHT: *A New Kind of Woman*, 1929, directed by Heinosuke Gosho, with Shizue Takita (left) and Hikaru Yamanouchi. ABOVE: *Revue Sisters*, 1929, directed by Yasujiro Shimazu, with Sotaro Okada (left) and Yukichi Iwata. RIGHT: *What Made Her Do It?*, 1930, directed by Shigeyoshi Suzuki, with Kaku Hamada (left) and Keiko Takatsu.

More subtle (and consequently somewhat less popular) were those Mizoguchi films which, taking the same theme, insisted less explicitly, and therefore all the more strongly, that the poor were being victimized by the exploiting rich. One of these was the poetic *Nihonbashi*. Another was *And Yet They Go On*, a very strong film which showed what society did to a mother and daughter forced into prostitution. Even more subtle were a series of Ozu comedies in which this glaring imbalance of power and money were treated to sarcasm and ridicule rather than polemic. *I Graduated, But...* showed the fate (horrid, then as now) of the Japanese graduate, his mind full of John Stuart Mill, who suddenly comes face to face with Japanese economic reality in the form of an eight-hour day and a white-collar job. The feeling was much the same as that prevailing in other countries and showing up in pictures like *One More Spring*, and *Brother, Can You Spare a Dime*. The difference lay in the polemic of a director like Shigeyoshi Suzuki and the subtlety of a director like Yasujiro Ozu. Both perfectly expressed, in their various ways, the temper of the times.

TOP: Kenji Mizoguchi on the set for *Hometown*, 1929, with Shizue Natsukawa (left) and Yoshie Fujiwara (right). CENTER: *And Yet They Go On*, 1931, directed by Kenji Mizoguchi, with Reiji Ichiki (left) and Yoko Umemura.

BY 1931 the Japanese cinema was thirty-five years old and was just attaining a maturity which made it the equal of any cinema. Late because of the stage orientation of both audience and production, because of the lasting influence of the *benshi*, and because of a national timidity which likes what it already knows, the art of the motion picture in Japan grew into one which, more than most, explicated life as it is rather than as it should be. Japanese directors (Ozu, Mizoguchi, Ito, a few others) had also realized that one of the wonders of cinema is that it can move, can make one feel, can approximate that great philosophical goal: empathy. For these reasons, character, in the best Japanese films, is rarely sacrificed to the exigencies of the "well-constructed plot," and cinematic technique is reserved solely to its proper service of making a film emotionally comprehensible. This experiment involves both trial and error, but by 1931 the Japanese cinema showed that distinctive profile which the West has come to recognize.

Then, as in other countries, sound struck. The revolution was not so complete and chaotic as in other lands because in Japan, there had always been sound—the drone of the *benshi*. Paradoxically, therefore, the arrival

ABOVE: Among those regarding the microphone are Yoshinobu Ikeda (left), Hideo Fujino (center in white), Den Ohinata and Sumiko Kurishima (right). RIGHT: *The Neighbor's Wife and Mine*, 1931, directed by Heinosuke Gosho, with (from left) Hideko Takamine, Atsushi Watanabe and Kinuyo Tanaka.

of real sound meant a freedom from sound. *Benshi* banished, the film could revel in especially recorded silence. The first talkie was Gosho's *The Neighbor's Wife and Mine,* a delightful comedy about a social situation—a hardworking husband, a traditional and neglected wife, a jazzy "modern girl" next door—and had very little talk in it. That the jazzy girl likes jazz occasioned the music in the film; that wife and husband are on the outs occasioned most of the silence. Sound when used was used inventively: the mewing of a kitten gets the husband up at night; sounds of next-door revelry accompany the pantomimed fury of the wife; the sleepy whining of the child is aural counterpoint to the almost wordless arguments—fierce stares, tossings of heads—of husband and wife. From the first, the Japanese understood the resources of sound. America and France were making talky stage-plays on film, and Japan made a delicately muted comedy which, as one Japanese critic has said, "remained within cinematic traditions and borrowed none from the stage.... [Gosho] knew from the first that film must always be film and must not attempt to be recorded theater."

41

ABOVE: *Young Miss*, 1931, directed by Yasujiro Ozu, with (from left) Tokihiko Okada, Sumiko Kurishima, and Tatsuo Saito. RIGHT: *Chorus of Tokyo*, 1931, directed by Yasujiro Ozu, with (from left) Kenji Oyama, Tokihiko Okada and Tatsuo Saito.

As THE FIRST talkie (Gosho's film) had indicated, the coming of sound meant, in Japan at any rate, a new lightness, a new relaxation. Sound meant music as well as dialogue; it meant freedom from the exigencies of a purely visual plot; it meant, in short, a happier kind of picture. The silent film in all countries had demonstrated that it is easier to be tragic than comic. René Clair, Chaplin, Lubitsch, Keaton, Laurel and Hardy were exceptions, and their pictures are exceptional because they manage to be both silent and funny. The Japanese silent film had, more often than not, tragic intentions. There were, however, other reasons for this as well. One of them was that, though the prime influence on Japanese film was the American motion picture, during the late 1920's the more somber of the German UFA products became greatly admired, partially because they were indeed so somber, and in Japan, as in postwar Germany, life was often somber. A simpler reason for admiration was that the UFA productions sold very well all over the world and were, at the same time, critically admired. This the Japanese were not long in noticing. They are never long in noticing success. In the Meiji period, for example, the Japanese army had begun to pattern itself after the French. Just then the Franco-Prussian War occurred; the Germans won. And that is why the Japanese army is built after the German pattern, and a relic of the period remains in the black, high-collar uniforms of Japanese students, originally based on Prussian cadet costumes. That the Germans won was quite enough to convince the Japanese of the innate superiority of their army. In the same way, the UFA's success all over the world made the Japanese anxious to simulate the tone of these productions, and this meant a predominance of earnest and searching tragedy.

A more important reason for the tragic bent of the Japanese film—and the notorious predilection of the Japanese for the unhappy ending—is philosophical. Tragedy presumes a closed world, a contained place where values are known and recognized, where ideas are commonly accepted. Kabuki tragedy and Stuart tragedy can exist only where this premise exists—in Tokugawa Japan or in Cavalier England. Historically, the Tokugawa period (1600–1867) was a completely closed world, both ordered and finite. The kabuki tragedy is usually based on the idea that duty and inclination

Scenes from *I Was Born, But...*, 1932, directed by Yasujiro Ozu, with Hideo Sugawara and Tokkan-kozo (photo above).

are incompatible. Their opposition can only resolve itself in either murder or suicide, and either of these alternatives is sufficiently tragic. While it is tragic to believe that what one would like to do and what one ought to do are hopelessly far apart, it is at the same time reassuring because it clearly defines one's choice. It seems especially comforting on the stage (or screen) because this simplification can suggest that there is nothing more than this to life, that one now knows the worst. Tragedy appears particularly consoling now, when there is no more ordered cosmos and when the universe expands into endless alternative. The West clings to its *Hamlet* just as Japan clutches at its *Forty-seven Ronin*. In an age such as this, when art labors and produces nothing more than *The Death of a Salesman*, the tragic is held particularly dear. For the same reason, the Japanese clutches the unhappy ending because this, at least, offers a kind of security.

Japan, which remains in many ways feudal enough to suggest a closed and finite world, prefers, perhaps more than some countries, tragedy to the alternative, chaos. Yet, as we have seen, it is just the fortuitous, the chaotic, the meaninglessness of life which the camera can and must reflect. It is at its most persuasive just when it is reflecting the accidental, the unplanned. Flaherty's "slight narrative" and the opened-ended stories which some directors prefer preserve the accidental meaninglessness but, at the same time, impose a slight order on the events to be shown. This is a compromise which Japan was to learn, eventually better than any other country, but application took time. Further, Japanese film could learn little from the stage. It is almost exclusively tragic and prefers the same, finite even though unhappy world to the accidental, fortuitous, chaotic but perhaps happy world of reality. One might even say that tragedy is equated with death in a way deeper than is commonly supposed: the tragic view of the world implies no change and therefore no life; reality is not like this, and one of the triumphs of tragedy is that it imposes itself in the very face of reality. Cinema, on the other hand, is connected with life, with reality. It can't help but be. (And George Sadoul has pointed out that the very names of the early machines— the Vitascope, for example—had to do with "life.")

The history of the film in Japan is, in part, the spectacle of a death-oriented people, people holding a tragic view of life, turning toward and confronting in their own way the chaos of living. In the films of Ozu, of Naruse, of Mizoguchi one later finds an acceptance of the fortuitous, a "life is like that" smile, which is as beautiful as it is useful. First, however, Japanese film had to break itself of seeing things in terms of the finite and the tragic.

One of the alternatives of the tragic is the comic, and though there are many shadings in between, it was rather Japanese of Japan to run to the other end of the gamut and begin producing screen comedies, with not a tragedy in sight. To be sure, comedy had already evolved in Japan (though not at all to the extent it had in the West) and among these were the films of Ozu. He did not make use of sound until later, but his films of this period nonetheless reflect the freedom which he and other directors were feeling. Having made the wry *I Graduated, But...*, he continued, in 1931, with the charming nonsense-comedy *Young Miss*, and the very amusing *Chorus of Tokyo*. In 1932 he made a masterpiece in *I Was Born, But....* Two small boys, their father and mother, move into a new neighborhood. One of their playmates is the son of their father's boss. At his house they look at home movies where the father, to please his employer, acts the fool. The boys, shocked and hurt, decide to have no more to do with him; they go on a hunger-strike. They cannot understand why it is that if they can so easily beat up the boss's son, their father should so demean himself before their playmate's father. They are protesting against what they cannot yet know is one of the great inequalities of life. But they are young, they get hungry; they forget, they eat. Life goes on, and they will probably in turn behave much as their father has. The fact that life goes on, that one emerges even from the most damaging of experiences—this is a telling choice between those stronger emotions which insist upon the tragic and those which demand the comic. Ozu deliberately tells his story as a light comedy in which nothing ends. By treating a serious subject lightly he avoids the theatrical; by making a comic film out of at least potentially tragic material he creates within us a smiling if painful acceptance. We accept life as it is and find beauty in the order of things as they really are, which is a very different thing from finding solace in an order merely presumed.

Scenes from *I Was Born, But...*, with Tatsuo Saito, Tokkan-kozo and Hideo Sugawara.

44

TOP, LEFT TO RIGHT: *The Revenge Champion*, 1931, directed by Tomu Uchida, with Denjiro Okochi (left) and Takeko Sakuma; *The Loyal Forty-seven Ronin*, 1932, directed by Teinosuke Kinugasa, with Kotaro Bando (left) and Akiko Chihaya; *The Life of Bangoku*, 1932, directed by Sadao Yamanaka, with Isuzu Yamada (left) and Denjiro Okochi. CENTER LEFT: *Peerless Patriot*, 1932, directed by Mansaku Itami, with Chiezo Kataoka (left) and Isuzu Yamada. RIGHT: *Travels Under the Blue Sky*, 1932, directed by Hiroshi Inagaki, with Chiezo Kataoka (left) and Kunio Tamura (center). BOTTOM: *The Sedge Hat*, 1932, directed by Hiroshi Inagaki, with Chiezo Kataoka.

SOUND, THEN, not only helped films away from the presumed tragic, it also showed that heroics need not be empty. In a silent picture the hero—perfectly silent—often attracts because, since he does not speak, we can never be sure of his motivations and hence attribute to him all manner of fascination. In a talkie, the man had better have something interesting to say or else we are disappointed. Our preference is indicated by the continued convention of the uncommunicative hero, the strong and silent man (Gary Cooper, Toshiro Mifune). If he talks too much then he ceases to be heroic because we understand him too well. But there is another (and sounder) way to make a hero, and that is to celebrate his humanity. In that case, however, he cannot merely grab his gun or sling his sword. He must have reasons for what he does, and this means that he must have a real character. After the arrival of sound, even such near-legendary heros as Chuji Kunisada and the entire

45

cast of *The Loyal Forty-seven Ronin* became quite human. Denjiro Okochi in *The Revenge Champion*, and Chiezo Kataoka in *Peerless Patriot* sliced and cut, but they were now thinking, feeling men. In *The Sedge Hat* and *Travels Under the Blue Sky*, Hiroshi Inagaki created a new kind of hero (seen in finished form in the much later *Samurai*) who even lost occasionally. Kenji Mizoguchi, in pictures like *Meiji Samurai*, put his anti-heroes in the midst of a wonderfully living and acutely detailed past, and Sadao Yamanaka, the greatest of all Japanese period-film directors, created in such films as *Road to Uminari* and *The Life of Bangoku* a modern hero in the thoughtful samurai who fights when he has to, but whose worst enemy is the poverty which makes him commit action considered unthinkable in the old period film: he sells his sword in order to eat.

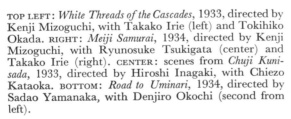
TOP LEFT: *White Threads of the Cascades*, 1933, directed by Kenji Mizoguchi, with Takako Irie (left) and Tokihiko Okada. RIGHT: *Meiji Samurai*, 1934, directed by Kenji Mizoguchi, with Ryunosuke Tsukigata (center) and Takako Irie (right). CENTER: scenes from *Chuji Kunisada*, 1933, directed by Hiroshi Inagaki, with Chiezo Kataoka. BOTTOM: *Road to Uminari*, 1934, directed by Sadao Yamanaka, with Denjiro Okochi (second from left).

46

TOP RIGHT: Teinosuke Kinugasa directing a scene in 1933. CENTER LEFT: *Our Neighbor, Miss Yae*, 1934, directed by Yasujiro Shimazu, with Yumeko Aizome (left) and Sanae Takasugi. RIGHT: *Duckweed Story*, 1934, directed by Yasujiro Ozu, with Emiko Yakumo (left) and Takeshi Sakamoto.

SOUND ALSO contributed greatly to the already detailed realism of the *shomin-geki*, that genre of films about middle-class life which had become so important a part of Japanese cinema. The West has no precise equivalent. A film like *Rocco e suo fratelli* has the milieu, *Our Daily Bread* has the characterization, *Due soldi di speranza* has the comedy, and Sam Wood's *Our Town* has the mood. But even if the West has nothing like it, it got to see one of the best and earliest sound examples when Mikio Naruse's *Wife, Be Like a Rose* was shown in New York under the title of *Kimiko*. A poetry-writing mother and daughter live together and alone because the husband has gone to the country to live with a less demanding woman. The daughter sets out to visit him. Little-miss-fix-it, the girl is going to bring him home with her. But once there she finds him happy, a very good husband, and a fine father to her half-brother and sister. She realizes that things are more complicated than she had thought. It is not so simple as that father is bad, or that mother is bad. She returns to the city newly aware that people are what they are and that anything we do—mother writing poetry, father living with another

47

woman—to make life livable, we do because we must. Mark Van Doren, writing in *The Nation*, said: "...the film contains a new experience for us... which comes from the whole management of the story...and I can suggest this difference best by saying that...the narrative is presented with a simplicity and a seriousness, and a certainty of effect, which reminds us of something too frequently forgotten in the movies, namely, that economy is power.... The result is one of the most moving films I know."

Naruse, Ozu, Shimazu, and Mizoguchi in the films of this period (and later) find that tragedy (father as villain) is both too convenient and too dishonest. Life is more complicated than this, and this is what Naruse suggests by showing us the face of the girl as she begins to say what her mother had told her to say, then stops when she realizes that words are inadequate. One of the triumphs of Japanese sound-film is that following scene where the girl and her father's common-law wife look at each other, realize that words cannot express their humanly mixed feelings, and both burst into tears.

CENTER: scenes from *Wife, Be Like a Rose*, with (from left) Sachiko Chiba, Kamatari Fujiwara; Tomoko Ito, Chiba and Heihachiro Okawa. BOTTOM LEFT: *Okoto and Sasuke*, 1935, directed by Yasujiro Shimazu, with Kokichi Takada (left) and Kinuyo Tanaka. RIGHT: *Field Poppy*, 1935, directed by Kenji Mizoguchi, with Kuniko Miyake (left).

TOP LEFT: *The Izu Dancer*, 1935, directed by Heinosuke Gosho, with Kinuyo Tanaka (left) and Den Ohinata. RIGHT: *Daibosatsu Pass*, 1935, directed by Hiroshi Inagaki, with Fujiko Fukamizu (left) and Denjiro Okochi. CENTER: *Kakita Akanishi*, 1936, directed by Mansaku Itami, with Shosaku Sugiyama (left) and Chiezo Kataoka.

ANOTHER reason for the strong interest in character in the Japanese film of this period—other than necessities of sound and the interest in the middle classes as real, feeling people—was that the rise of military power, the widening chasm between a well-intentioned Cabinet and a dangerously aggressive army and navy clique, had made the personal, the subjective, worth saving. The common Tokugawa mode of thought was "we," the secure collective which feudalism prescribes and exists upon. During the Showa period (and before), "I" became a way of thinking. Japanese literature had been insisting upon this for some time, and then as now one of the most common literary forms was the *shishōsetsu*, the first-person novel. During the 1930's there were more *shishōsetsu* than ever, and the films found in them a major source of material. Yasunari Kawabata's *The Izu Dancer* was made into a charming and nostalgic film by Heinosuke Gosho; *Daibosatsu Pass*, a best-seller, made the first of its many screen appearances in a picture by Hiroshi Inagaki. Though this particular literary form preserves the subjective, it has been argued that it does little else, and there is the general feeling that the *shishōsetsu* limits literature as literature. Perhaps it need not. Still, Japan has nothing like that greatest of all *shishōsetsu*, Marcel Proust's novel. Japanese authors tend to turn the form into a confessional, and the interest consequently becomes biographical. It is unavoidable that a kind of pleasant shallowness is the result. Movies, if made from books, however, thrive on just this lack of depth. Since films can only show the surface of things, books which do the same thing are particularly fine vehicles. The cinema cannot approximate the depth of a great novel, but the "living" quality of film can completely animate a book which has no depth at all. *The Magnificent Ambersons* made an excellent film, and *Moby Dick*, as several directors have demonstrated, cannot be made into a movie. Japanese literature is of such loose construction, is in itself often so inconclusive, that what may appear a very slight novella makes a most convincing film. Such novels include the fortuitous, the "open-ended," the inconclusive, which is the very stuff of cinema. Films such as Ozu's *Duckweed Story*, Shimazu's *Our Neighbor, Miss Yae* and *Okoto and Sasuke* (taken from a Junichiro Tanizaki novella about a blind *koto* player and her servant) and Mizoguchi's *Field Poppy* and *Osaka Elegy* are extremely rich in incident and episode, and almost devoid of what (in a novel) would hold our interest: the story, or the plot. The latter film is a picture (one hesitates to say a story) of a girl who is confronted with the two ways of the Japanese: the traditional and the modern. Many small episodes show her reactions, and at the end (there is no conclusion) she still confronts what she chooses to see as a dilemma.

CENTER LEFT: *Million Ryo Money Pot*, 1935, directed by Sadao Yamanaka, with Kiyomi (left) and Denjiro Okochi. RIGHT: *The Village Tattooed Man*, 1935, directed by Sadao Yamanaka, with Fujiko Fukamizu (left) and Chojuro Kawarazaki. BOTTOM LEFT: *The Gorge between Love and Hate*, 1936, directed by Kenji Mizoguchi, with Seizaburo Kawazu (left) and Fumiko Yamaji. RIGHT: *Osaka Elegy*, 1936, directed by Kenji Mizoguchi, with (from left) Eitaro Shindo, Isuzu Yamada, and Kensaku Hara.

50

Sisters of the Gion, 1936, directed by Kenji Mizoguchi.
ABOVE: Yoko Umemura (left) and Isuzu Yamada.
RIGHT: Isuzu Yamada.

MIZOGUCHI's *Sisters of the Gion* has somewhat the same theme and is even more episodic. There are two sisters: the elder is a geisha; the younger is an apprentice who, though living in the traditional geisha section of Kyoto, dreams of a job in Tokyo, of getting married. Though there is an eventual automobile accident, there is no plot. We come to understand that the elder will continue in her traditional ways because they are sustaining at the same time that they are self-defeating; the younger will always have before her this vision of a self which perhaps will never be realized but which is necessary for her. The two sisters are equated and the opposites are both revealed as necessary.

51

TOP LEFT: *Theater of Life*, 1936, directed by Tomu Uchida, with Isamu Kosugi (left) and Reizaburo Yamamoto (right). RIGHT: *I Am a Cat*, 1936, directed by Yasujiro Shimazu, with Sadao Maruyama (center). CENTER: *Young People*, 1937, directed by Shiro Toyoda, with (standing, from left) Shizue Natsukawa, Den Ohinata and Haruyo Ichikawa foreground.

UCHIDA's *Theater of Life* and Shimazu's *I Am a Cat* (the latter based on the episodic comic novel by Soseki Natsume) are equally concerned with character and little else. In fact, as Japanese literature has indicated, to be truly concerned with character means that you cannot use it (for to use is to misuse) in making a plot. In the Shimazu film there is no story at all. We are presented instead with a fine gallery of "types," including as hero a Japanese intellectual, all ideas and no action, his balding wife, his pedantic and donnish university-professor friend who wears bow ties and likes to quote from Hegel. Again, in films such as Mizoguchi's *The Gorge Between Love and Hate*, Uchida's *The Naked Town*, and Kumagai's *Many People*, we are given pregnant episodes during which character is revealed. This is not the rule in Japanese cinema any more than it is anywhere else, and there are many such films as Shimazu's curious *Light of Asakusa* with its overtones of a plot-heavy *Carmen*, and the first Japanese co-production, *The New Earth*, which can be said to have had a real plot, insofar as the heroine throws herself into a volcano, at least in the version shown abroad as *Daughter of the Samurai*. Nonetheless, the Japanese lack of interest in film-plot is so pronounced that it never occurs to them to miss it. In the West, a picture like *The Crowd*, *The Salvation Hunters*, *L'Avventura* or *Muriel* is considered completely exceptional. During this period, then, when the military was looking askance at all liberal opinion, when it became suspicious to have too individual a personality, when a highly plot-conscious propaganda office was already being formed, film after film appeared which dignified the human character by showing it in its unique richness and all but plot-proof complication.

TOP: *Children in the Wind*, 1937, directed by Hiroshi Shimizu, with Masao Hayama (left) and Bakudan-kozo. CENTER: *The Naked Town*, 1937, directed by Tomu Uchida, with Chieko Murata (left) and Koji Shima. BOTTOM: *The Light of Asakusa*, 1937, directed by Yasujiro Shimazu, with Chishu Ryu (left) and Ken Uehara.

LEFT: *Many People*, 1937, directed by Hisatora Kumagai, with Koji Shima and Sadako Sawamura (center foreground). BELOW LEFT: *The New Earth*, 1937, directed by Mansaku Itami and Arnold Fank, with Setsuko Hara. BELOW: *The Summer Battle of Osaka*, 1937, directed by Teinosuke Kinugasa.

IT IS PERHAPS singular that during these years when the military was carrying emperor, Cabinet, and people directly into total war, the period film (that feudal remain) should have become an anti-feudal, anti-heroic genre which humanized the hero and championed the individual. The main reason that this could occur was that the period film had come a long way from its Matsunosuke beginnings and, during the late 1920's, had even become a vehicle for social criticism. Kinugasa's *The Summer Battle of Osaka*; Sotoji Kimura's *Shinsengumi*, about the fall of the Tokugawa Shogunate; Kumagai's *The Abé Clan*, and Takizawa's *The Robber Saga*—all were personal and anti-heroic in that the hero's problems (to a greater or lesser degree) were both moral and ethical. So popular (during this period of brutal war in China and ruthless conquest in Manchuria) was this humanization of the feudal that the popular comedian Enoken made a number of parodies, among them *Enoken, the Priest,* which, under the disguise of period comedy, made all manner of fun of the "warrior spirit."

54

RIGHT: *Shinsengumi*, 1937, directed by Sotoji Kimura, with Kanemon Nakamura (foreground kneeling) and Chojuro Kawarazaki (standing). BELOW: *The Robber Saga*, 1937, directed by Eisuke Takizawa, with Kanemon Nakamura (third from left).

THE GREATEST of all period-film directors was Sadao Yamanaka. In films such as *The Million-Ryo Money Pot*, *The Village Tattooed Man*, and—one of the most important movies of its time—the 1937 picture, *Humanity and Paper Balloons*, his last film, he searched for human values in the inhuman Tokugawa era. In the latter film, for example, his samurai has already sold his sword for rice and his wife must work—making paper balloons for sale. Already, then, two things have occurred which the samurai code does not allow. Then he accidentally involves himself in a kidnapping and has the humanity to shelter a man wanted by the military authorities. From this act of kindness and friendship comes his death. This movie was made in the year that the Japanese took Nanking with a show of inhumanity all but unprecedented in modern times. Director Yamanaka was drafted shortly after the picture was released, was sent to China as a common soldier and was killed in battle a year later.

55

Humanity and Paper Balloons, 1937, directed by Sadao
Yamanaka. TOP TO BOTTOM: (from left foreground)
Sukezo Suketakaya, Chojuro Kawarazaki, and Kanemon Nakamura; (from left) Kanemon Nakamura, Emi-
taro Nakamura, and Daisuke Kato; Kanemon Nakamura. BOTTOM: last photograph of Director Yamanaka.

56

LEFT: *Eno-ken, the Priest*, 1938, directed by Torajiro Saito, with Kenichi Enomoto (center). ABOVE: *The Abe Clan*, 1938, directed by Hisatora Kumagai, with Kanemon Nakamura (right).

A SAFER WAY to continue to make films about real people and real problems during a time when human values were being turned to use by the state was to film famous novels or to make films about children. The Japanese, like most people, reserve their finest and most selfless emotions for their young. Further, they (who so often see each other as replaceable units in a social structure) have a strong feeling, amounting to a mystique, that a child (particularly their own) is a unique personality, an irreplaceable entity. The mistreatment of a child is a crime and when it occurs brings more tears than even Dickens would have believed possible. Hiroshi Shimizu in *Children in the Wind* began a whole series in which, as in the Ozu films about children, the trusting world of the young was favorably contrasted with the corrupt world of adults. Tasaka's *A Pebble by the Wayside* (as hardy a perennial as *Oliver Twist* and later to be remade and remade again), showed a child forced to make his way alone in the cold world of grown-ups. Kajiro Yamamoto's somewhat slick *Composition Class* and Shiro Toyoda's very tender *Crybaby Apprentice* were about children whom the adults are too busy to want. In the latter picture, the little boy is shifted from relatives to friends and is finally permanently misplaced. When he returns home to find the house empty, his mother run off with her boyfriend, this age of official indifference and jingoistic nationalism melted, and people still talk about how much they cried during it.

TOP TO BOTTOM: *A Pebble by the Wayside*, 1938, directed by Tomotaka Tasaka, with Isamu Kosugi (standing) and Akihiko Katayama (second from right); *Composition Class*, 1938, directed by Kajiro Yamamoto, with Hideko Takamine (left standing); *Crybaby Apprentice*, 1938, directed by Shiro Toyoda, with Mitsugu Fuji (left) and Yumeko Aizome; *Nightingale*, 1938, directed by Shiro Toyoda, with Haruko Sugimura (center).

TOP LEFT: *Older Brother, Younger Sister*, 1939, directed by Yasujiro Shimazu, with Sadao Maruyama (left) and Heihachi Okawa. RIGHT: *Warm Current*, 1939, directed by Kozaburo Yoshimura, with Shin Saburi (left) and Mieko Takamine. LEFT: *Four Seasons of Children*, 1939, directed by Hiroshi Shimizu.

MANY OF THE humanistic films of this uneasy period were based on famous novels, the feeling being that a classic novel could not be readily criticized. Tasaka's film about the little boy was based on a Yuzo Yamamoto novel. Toyoda's picture was after a famous novel by Fumiko Hayashi, and his earlier *Young People*, about a schoolgirl who gets a crush on her teacher, was taken from a Yojiro Ishizaka story. Yoshimura's *Warm Current*, a film about a hospital superintendent and two nurses, was from a Kunio Kishida novel, and Shimazu's *Elder Brother, Younger Sister* was able to obliquely criticize the family system because the original was so well known. In *Nightingale*, Toyoda presented a picture of life in rural Japan which contained not one note of moral "up-lift." He was able to do this, was able to interest himself only in character, because the film was based on a highly episodic and highly popular novel by the famous Einosuke Ito.

59

LEFT: *Mud and Soldiers*, 1939, directed by Tomotaka Tasaka, with Isamu Kosugi (right). BELOW LEFT AND RIGHT: *Five Scouts*, 1939, directed by Tomotaka Tasaka, with Isamu Kosugi.

EVEN THE first films about the war itself, though made directly for the Ministry of Propaganda, were distinguished by a concern for human character, for the meticulous rendering of milieu, and for an absence of plot which, during the 1930's, Japan had made the most important elements of a cinematic style. Tasaka's *Five Scouts* is the story of five men who are sent to reconnoiter. Only four return—then the fifth also returns safely. At the end of the picture there is the call for a general attack, and this time we know that not one of them will return. In *Mud and Soldiers,* a recurring image is that of soldiers struggling in a long march which seems endless, seems without goal; incidents are imbedded within this march, and the director's only concern is for the character of the men, their various ways of reacting. Such a movie is usually found in the postwar cinema of a country, very rarely in the prewar film. And this was among the last of such dedicated and humanistic pictures about war.

60

Earth, 1939, directed by Tomu Uchida. TOP: Akiko Kazami. RIGHT: Isamu Kosugi (left) and Bontaro Miyake. LEFT: Kaichi Yamamoto (left) and Akiko Kazami (right).

ONE OF THE finest films of the decade and, in its way, a summation of all that the Japanese cinema had come to represent during the 1930's, was Tomu Uchida's *Earth*. In both *Theater of Life* and *The Naked Town*, the director had shown middle-class life in a way which was in itself an oblique attack on the values of a materialistic society. In *Earth* he made a film about farmers—peasants, really, since a feudal system of land tenure was maintained until after the war—and wanted to show the difficulties of ignorance and poverty under which these people struggled. He also wanted to make a real documentary which would show the cycle of the seasons and would indicate both the sorrows and the joys of life necessarily close to nature. To do this, he used only the slightest of stories. A farmer loses all of his money, is driven nearly to despair, yet manages to find new hope. What the hope consists of Uchida is careful not to say, since he did not subscribe to the theory that collective farming solves all agrarian ills. His film was no call to revolution. It was rather a statement, even a poetic one. The snows slowly melt, new leaves appear, it is summer, then the leaves fall. Against this natural background the farmers live and work and hope, and there seems an equation between these two cycles. The West's closest approximation to this film is Roquier's *Farrébique*, except that the Japanese film relied even less on plot and more on visuals.

61

The vision of the Japanese, their ways of seeing things, has occasionally been commented upon. Tending to see nature as a form of art, the Japanese eye usually selects an element to stand for the whole (the bamboo grove in this film, the solitary tree in *Horse*); composition (the placement of lake and tree in the picnic scene of *Ugetsu*, for example) insists that the natural dominate the eye, and repeated scenes (the rushes in Mizoguchi's *Sansho*) emphasize these natural elements until a feeling very near reality is reached. To be sure, the main reason that nature looks real in a Japanese film is because it *is* real. When a river becomes as real as those in *L'Atalante* or *Il Grido*, we remark upon it; the complete reality of the bamboo grove and its use in reflecting the emotions of the characters in *Earth*, however, were thought in no way remarkable by the Japanese; rather, they were thought fitting. If you take a walk along the seashore with a Japanese girl, she may point to a single pine and say that she feels like that tree looks, and you are to *feel* whether she means lonely as the pine, or proudly solitary as the pine. This interrelation between people and nature and the peculiar way in which they (inventors of the pathetic fallacy) see themselves reflected in it are a part of everyday life and consequently find a place in the films. It is perhaps for this reason that even the largest companies and the poorest directors use real nature—why Uchida (small company, good director) actually spent a year on a farm creating his film. An all studio-shot film is extremely rare and is generally felt to be closed in—which, of course, it is.

The Japanese are visual-minded (in contrast to aural-minded) and this is insisted upon (if not created) by the written language and the way it is used. The written word carries ever so much more weight than the spoken, and one of the reasons for sparing use of sound (even now) in a Japanese film is the distrust of the spoken word. (It also creates very bad sound tracks and truly appalling dubbing, no one minding that sounds and lip movements do not synchronize.) In a film such as *Earth*, the people do not talk much; rather (like the girl on the beach), they are reflected by their surroundings, by the nature in which they live and work. The picture, as the title indicates, is about the elements: the elements of nature, the elements of humanity. It is in itself elemental and hence honest. By 1939 the Japanese had learned to reflect themselves in the mirror of cinema with a rare fidelity. This, however, was to be nearly the last of such artful and peaceful endeavors for some time. War, like plot, called for the *use* of humanity and not its elucidation.

Scene during the filming of *Earth*.

LEFT: *The Story of the Last Chrysanthemums*, 1939, directed by Kenji Mizoguchi, with (from left) Gonjuro Kawarazaki, Yoko Umemura, Shotaro Hanayagi and Yotaro Kawanami. BELOW: Scenes from *Woman of Osaka*, 1940, directed by Kenji Mizoguchi. LEFT: Ichiro Yuki (in rickshaw). RIGHT: Kinuyo Tanaka.

WITH JAPAN now fully committed to war, the Home Ministry laid down a code of instruction for the industry which, among other things, ordered that military matters were not to be made light of, and that scenes of corruption and excessive merriment were to be avoided. At the same time, tendencies toward individualism as expressed in American and European pictures were to be eliminated. Instead, the beauty of the indigenous family system and the spirit of complete sacrifice for the nation was to be developed. One of the more influential magazines came out with a manifesto which said that "dramatic art must forget the old invidualistic and class attitudes and must begin to realize that it has a cultural role to perform in the total program of our new national consciousness." One of the ways in which the better directors reacted to this was to escape. Kenji Mizoguchi (though he was later put to work making films under government orders) was among the first to find a somewhat precarious haven in the Meiji period where, in pictures such as *The Story of the Last Chrysanthemum* (about a kabuki actor) and *Woman of Osaka* (about the *bunraku* puppets), he could make hopefully

63

safe character studies. Upon retreating further into the Tokugawa, however, he was collared and made to create yet another version of the kabuki perennial, this one all for the war-effort and called *The Loyal Forty-seven Ronin of the Genroku Era*. Shiro Toyoda, on the other hand, managed for some time to ignore the war, as in *Spring on Leper's Island*, the story of a dedicated woman in a leper colony which represented one call for compassion in an age marching into destruction. It is always easier to join than to stand against (particularly in Japan), and consequently there were a number of pictures like *China Night*, the story of a love affair between a Chinese orphan and a Japanese naval officer. There were three endings made for this particular movie. The ending for Chinese use shows them happily wed; the Southeast Asian ending shows him saving her from suicide; the ending for Japan allows her to go on and kill herself.

ABOVE: *Spring on Leper's Island*, 1940, directed by Shiro Toyoda, with Shizue Natsukawa (right). RIGHT: *China Night*, 1940, directed by Osamu Fushimizu, with Yoshiko Yamaguchi (left) and Tamae Kiyokawa (right).

64

LEFT TOP TO BOTTOM: Scenes from *The Story of Tank Commander Nishizumi*, 1940, directed by Kozaburo Yoshimura, with Ken Uehara and Takeshi Sakamoto. RIGHT: *The Burning Sky*, 1940, directed by Yutaka Abe, with Katsuhiko Haida (left) and Den Ohinata.

THERE WERE other ways of making war films, however. Kozaburo Yoshimura's *The Story of Tank Commander Nishizumi* managed to satisfy the military and still reflect, though somewhat dimly, the prewar humanistic ideal. His picture shows the tank commander being friendly with enemy civilians and, even worse, fraternizing with his own men. More typical was *The Burning Sky*, which showed officers being friendly only with each other, and *Navy*, a big production about the naval flyers who had bombed Pearl Harbor. Though earlier Makino pictures about the grand old feudal days would have been welcomed, the individual and sophisticated creations of Yamanaka, Itami, and Ito were considered highly dangerous to military ideals. The period film was officially frowned upon; but there were at least several. One of them was the younger Makino's *The Man Who Disappeared Yesterday*, which was relatively free of topical connotations. Another was Inagaki's *The Last Days of Edo*, which seemed made to order for the Home Office. In it the hero goes about instantly converting all rebels and dissidents to the emperor's side.

65

TOP: *The Last Days of Edo*, 1941, directed by Hiroshi Inagaki, with Tsumasaburo Bando (center). CENTER LEFT: *Navy*, 1941, directed by Tomotaka Tasaka, with Takashi Shimura (left) and Akira Yamanouchi. RIGHT: *The Man Who Disappeared Yesterday*, 1941, directed by Masahiro Makino, with Kazuo Hasegawa (lower right) and Isuzu Yamada (center).

Horse, 1941, directed by Kajiro Yamamoto. LEFT: scenes with Hideko Takamine. RIGHT: (from left) Shoji Kiyokawa, Takamine and Kamatari Fujiwara.

KAJIRO YAMAMOTO's *Horse* would have been an unusual film whenever it had appeared. That it appeared in 1941 is surprising indeed. One of the reasons —and one of the reasons that this gentle and pastoral picture was one of the great wartime hits—was that it marked a return to what many thought the proper business of the motion picture. Appearing among a vast majority of jingoistic, contrived, unentertaining films, it was a near-documentary which chronicled the seasons and showed the Japanese family as it really was. The only wartime concession was that the colt which the girl so carefully raises is to be a pack animal in the army; still, her tears as it joined the hundreds of other animals for the march to the port could have done little for the war effort. Yamamoto and his assistant, Akira Kurosawa, worked for over a year on this peaceful film which was all about animals, nature, and a little girl growing up. The celebrated contradictions of the Japanese character are well shown in that this peaceful movie was made in the year of Pearl Harbor.

Other directors, as well, still managed to avoid forgetting "the old individualistic...attitude." Among them was Yoshimura, who disregarded national policy entirely in his *South Wind*, a comedy subtly critical of the wartime new-rich. In *New Snow*, Gosho was even more daring. He took a script which was intended to be a national-policy drama about a soldier giving up his love for the greater love of country, and turned it into a nicely sentimental melodrama which only happened to occur during wartime.

ABOVE LEFT: *South Wind*, 1942, directed by Kozaburo Yoshimura, with Shin Saburi (left) and Chishu Ryu. ABOVE RIGHT: *New Snow*, 1942, directed by Heinosuke Gosho with Yumeji Tsukioka (left) and Michitaro Mizushima (center). RIGHT: Gosho (in front of camera) directing the scene.

EQUALLY FAR removed from the majority of Japanese wartime films was Ozu's *There Was a Father*, about a man's love for his son, how the son grows up and marries the daughter of his father's best friend. The beauty of the family system was shown (that is, the true beauty: the family helps its members, but does not particularly help its country); but, at the same time, as in all Ozu films, the beauty of individual character was also shown. Minoru Shibuya (the director who later, in 1965, completed the late Ozu's last film) showed a like interest in character in *That Woman*. Even such period spectaculars as Inagaki's three-part *Musashi Miyamoto* (fifteen years later to be remade by him as *Samurai*, winner of an Academy Award) managed to make his characters seem individual and real.

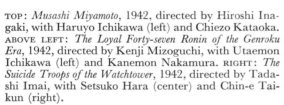

TOP: *Musashi Miyamoto*, 1942, directed by Hiroshi Ina-
gaki, with Haruyo Ichikawa (left) and Chiezo Kataoka.
ABOVE LEFT: *The Loyal Forty-seven Ronin of the Genroku
Era*, 1942, directed by Kenji Mizoguchi, with Utaemon
Ichikawa (left) and Kanemon Nakamura. RIGHT: *The
Suicide Troops of the Watchtower*, 1942, directed by Tada-
shi Imai, with Setsuko Hara (center) and Chin-e Tai-
kun (right).

TOP LEFT: *The War at Sea from Hawaii to Malaya*, 1942, directed by Kajiro Yamamoto, with (foreground from left) Susumu Fujita and Shoji Kiyokawa. RIGHT: *Generals and Soldiers*, 1942, directed by Tetsu Taguchi, with Tsumasaburo Bando (center). LEFT: *Attack on Singapore*, 1943, directed by Koji Shima.

NATURALLY, however, propaganda films outnumbered anything else, just as in America there were for a time more pictures like *The Purple Heart* than there were pictures like *Our Town*. Imai's *The Suicide Troops of the Watchtower* was just what the government ordered (including a willful confusion in labeling as "bandits" a guerilla army fighting for an independent Korea) but it is now something of an embarrassment to its makers, who managed to stop a proposed 1965 revival of the picture. *Attack on Singapore* was more of the same, as was *Generals and Soldiers*. Kajiro Yamamoto's *The War at Sea from Hawaii to Malaya* was to make up for the sins of *Horse* and, though the director used his excellent documentary techniques (along with studio shots so effective that Occupation authorities mistook them for newsreels of the real thing), the resulting picture was supposed to commemorate the first year of war against the United States (it was released on the anniversary of Pearl Harbor) and did, indeed, do merely that.

71

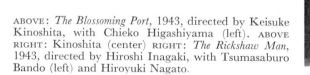

ABOVE: *The Blossoming Port*, 1943, directed by Keisuke Kinoshita, with Chieko Higashiyama (left). ABOVE RIGHT: Kinoshita (center) RIGHT: *The Rickshaw Man*, 1943, directed by Hiroshi Inagaki, with Tsumasaburo Bando (left) and Hiroyuki Nagato.

MORE remarkable than Yamamoto's making what was considered the most important national-policy film is that he *also* made *Horse*. The record of any Japanese director (including that of Mizoguchi) shows him satisfying the authorities and then, if possible, also making films which are close to nature, which capture the episodic nature of life, which insist upon atmosphere and mood—which, indeed, combine the strengths and the individuality of Japanese cinema. Most artists attempt this in wartime. They have little other choice. John Ford turns from *The Long Voyage Home* to *They Were Expendable*. Japanese directors do this sort of ideological somersault with more facility than most, however. Hiroshi Inagaki, having constructed his period spectacular and pleased the War Office, turned to the Meiji period and made his first version (his second, not nearly so good, won the Venice Prize in 1957) of *The Rickshaw Man*, and a new director, Keisuke Kinoshita, in *The Blossoming Port*, made his debut with a picture which, though based on a play sponsored by the Office of Public Information about the simple virtues of islanders making honest men of swindlers, managed to satirize the very wartime virtues it was presumably celebrating. Yet, no sooner was this done than the same director made at least several films which were all that the War Department could have desired.

72

Sanshiro Sugata, 1943, directed by Akira Kurosawa. Scenes from the film with TOP Susumu Fujita (kneeling), and Denjiro Okochi. BOTTOM RIGHT: Ryunosuke Tsukigata (with umbrella).

ANOTHER debut occurred at the same time—that of Akira Kurosawa. Having been an assistant director for Yamamoto, he was allowed in 1943 to make his first film. It was the story of the judo champion, Sanshiro Sugata, a fictionalized Meiji-period hero. The Office of Public Information liked the picture because it "showed the spirit of judo," and, by extension, Japan's valorous ways. Actually, it showed much more than this. It showed the individuality of its hero and, in this brilliantly realized debut film, Kurosawa's supreme individuality as an artist.

TOP LEFT: *Sanshiro Sugata—Part Two*, 1944, directed by Akira Kurosawa, with Ryunosuke Tsukigata (left), and Susumu Fujita. RIGHT: *The Most Beautiful*, 1944, directed by Akira Kurosawa, with Takako Irie (left) and Yoko Yaguchi. ABOVE: *The Life of an Artist*, 1944, directed by Kenji Mizoguchi, with Minosuke Bando (center) and Naritoshi Hayashi.

ITS SEQUEL, *Sanshiro Sugata—Part Two*, was even more gratefully received by the Office of Public Information, as well it might have been, being nothing but a jingoistic piece of hack work which was a parody of the original. In it the small but plucky judo champion is shown besting burly foreign boxers while a blue-eyed gallery gnashes its teeth. In good graces with the government, Kurosawa got his own way in his next picture. He wanted to make a documentary and he did so in *The Most Beautiful,* a record (using actresses but otherwise as unadorned as a newsreel) of girl workers in an optical-instruments factory which even now may be viewed as a realistic record of what the war effort really meant to the workers. After this, like Mizoguchi in *The Life of an Artist* and Gosho in *The Five-Storied Pagoda,* Kurosawa moved back to the Tokugawa period to create *They Who Step on the Tiger's Tail.*

74

TOP: *Five-storied Pagoda*, 1944, directed by Heinosuke Gosho with (from left) Ichijiro Oya, Eijiro Yanagi and Shotaro Hanayagi. BOTTOM: *They Who Step on the Tiger's Tail*, 1945, directed by Akira Kurosawa, with Kenichi Enomoto (left) and Denjiro Okochi.

They Who Step on the Tiger's Tail. LEFT: (from left, kneeling) Masayuki Mori, Takashi Shimura, Kenichi Enomoto, Denjiro Okochi (center, standing), and Susumu Fujita (right, sitting). BELOW LEFT: taking the scroll-reading scene, Kurosawa at camera viewfinder. RIGHT: the scroll-reading scene, Denjiro Okochi.

THIS hour-long film, completed just as the war was ending in 1945, was an almost literal adaptation of the kabuki *Kanjincho.* "Almost," because into this well-known story of feudal devotion, Kurosawa inserted one character not in the original. This was a porter played by the comedian Eno-ken (whose inclusion here is somewhat like putting Jerry Lewis in the cast of *Hamlet*), who not only does not understand what is happening but also fails to comprehend any of the feudal motivations which makes the characters do what they do. Cheerful, well-intentioned, he makes several of kabuki's most sublime moments completely irrelevant; he has much of the charm of Harpo Marx loose during *Il Trovatore.* The film was not released until 1953 because the Occupation authorities found what they called "feudal remnants" in it. If they had looked more closely, they would have seen that this is one of the strongest indictments of feudalism ever filmed.

LEFT: *Utamaro and His Five Women*, 1946, directed by Kenji Mizoguchi, with Toshiko Mizuka (left) and Minosuke Bando. BELOW LEFT: *Actress*, 1946, directed by Teinosuke Kinugasa, with Isuzu Yamada (left) and Hajime Izu. BELOW: *Lord for a Night*, 1946, directed by Teinosuke Kinugasa, with Denjiro Okochi (left) and Kazuo Hasegawa.

AFTER THE WAR, though half of the theaters in the major cities had been destroyed, the majority of the studios were intact. A week after the end of the war, the Japanese government decided that any theater able to get a program together could show it. The problem was that there were no films. No wartime pictures were to be shown at all, one of the first orders of the Allied Occupation having been that "national-policy" and military films were to be banned. To enforce this, a number of prints and negatives, including those of *Five Scouts* and *Musashi Miyamoto*, were ceremoniously burned by officers of the Eighth Army Headquarters. At the same time, a rigid censorship office was set up, one which rivaled the Japanese wartime Propaganda Office in its concern for meticulous bureaucratic detail. The reason that Kon Ichikawa's first picture, *A Girl at Dojo Temple*, has never been seen is that, since he had failed to apply for prior Occupation approval, screening permission was refused and the negative was taken. It became very difficult to make any kind of film, but some directors were more persuasive than others. Mizoguchi called on the officers and argued his case for

77

Utamaro and His Five Women. The artist Utamaro, he said, was a great cultural object, really a kind of pre-Occupation democrat in that he drew pictures of all classes of people, and that he treated women so well that it practically amounted to female emancipation. This latter subject was particularly dear to the heart of the Occupation and he was given permission. Kinugasa also wanted to make a comedy about feudal ways in *Lord for a Night*, but he faired less well. The authorities made him change the period from Tokugawa to Meiji, thus depriving the film of much of its bite. Later in the year both he and Mizoguchi hit on the same subject at the same time —the story of Sumako Matsui, an actress famed for her portrayal of Ibsen heroines, who committed suicide in 1918. Kinugasa's, called *Actress*, was the better of the two, but both were very hard on the social pressures said to be responsible for driving the actress to her destruction. That women need no longer destroy themselves was a lesson that the Occupation particularly wanted to teach, and it consequently encouraged a kind of love story which had never before been seen on the Japanese screen. This was the kind of film where the hero kisses the heroine in front of everyone in the audience. There was a real race to see which company would produce the first kiss. The winner was *A Certain Night's Kiss*, though the victorious did not really play fair. At the last moment, the director, Yasuke Chiba, lost his nerve and shot this long awaited scene half obscured by an open umbrella.

LEFT: *A Certain Night's Kiss*, 1946, directed by Yasuke Chiba, with Masao Wakahara (left) and Mitsue Nara.
ABOVE: *Those Who Make Tomorrow*, 1946, directed by Kajiro Yamamoto, Hideo Sakigawa and Akira Kurosawa, with Kenji Susukida (left) and Masao Shimizu.

TOP LEFT: *A Morning with the Osone Family*, 1946, directed by Keisuke Kinoshita, with (from left) Mitsuko Miura, Haruko Sugimura, Shiro Osaka. Shin Tokudaiji and Haruo Tanaka. RIGHT: *An Enemy of the People*, 1946, directed by Tadashi Imai, with Susumu Fujita (center). CENTER: *No Regrets for Our Youth*, 1946, directed by Akira Kurosawa, with Setsuko Hara (background) and Susumu Fujita.

MANY OF THE pictures of the postwar era were given over to a criticism of the old Japanese ways, rather than a celebration of the new ways of the Allies. Among these was Kinoshita's *A Morning with the Osone Family*, about a family during the war, the sons of which were either soldiers or else arrested for wartime political activities. With the peace (the "morning" referred to in the title) came hopes for a new life. Tadashi Imai, having so approved of what the army called "the Emperor's way" during the war, turned completely about and in *An Enemy of the People* strongly suggested that there was an imperial culprit, using this to make a strong stand for pro-Communist political action. Equally outspoken was the labor-union propaganda film called *They Who Make Tomorrow*, which was directed by Kajiro Yamamoto, Hideo Sekigawa, and Akira Kurosawa (the latter afterwards repudiated his part in it). It shows the old-fashioned father finally coming to understand the cause and eventually leading the workers, carrying the red flag and singing the *Internationale*.

79

AMONG THOSE films which examined the wartime conscience, by far the best was Kurosawa's *No Regrets for Our Youth*. In it a democratic teacher is silenced by the military. One of his students is jailed and later dies in prison. His daughter, married to the student, decides to leave her home and parents and go to live with her husband's mother and father, who are peasants. This she does in bravery and despair, knowing that she must somehow find meaning in her life. This solution, so stern, so personal, was quite different from that proposed by "everyone working together," an answer strongly suggested by both the Occupation and (for entirely different reasons) the Communist party. It was also one which (in Japan as elsewhere) meets with very little response. Like some other countries (and more than many), Japan is extremely fond of mass actions. It is the land where "togetherness" originated, and where a reaction like that of Kurosawa's heroine is absolutely atypical. And it is precisely for that reason, perhaps, that such extremely individual people as she should appeal. Certainly more typical is the Japanese who does something along with everyone else. When the American troops marched into the country, they were astonished to see the Japanese lining the roads, passive and orderly. This was the prime example of a mass action. The Emperor had told them that they had been misled for over a decade (the

TOP: *Four Love Stories* (*First Love*), 1947, directed by Shiro Toyoda, with (from center left) Ryo Ikebe and Yoshiko Kuga. CENTER LEFT: *The Fellows Who Ate the Elephant*, 1947, directed by Kozaburo Yoshimura, with Shinichi Himori (second from left). RIGHT: *The Record of a Tenement Gentleman*, 1947, directed by Yasujiro Ozu, with Choko Iida (left) and Reikichi Kawamura.

truth); and beyond this anyone could see that the Americans had won and to win is to be right. They were quite ready to put down their bamboo spears and start learning all about Lincoln. This precipitous about-face (neither the first nor the last in Japan's history) was just as sincere as had been the earlier all-out "war effort," and what we would call hypocrisy they would call practicability. On one day in August, 1945, everyone in Japan changed his mind. Now Japan was earnestly studying new ways and concerning itself with a new individuality. Thus it found attractive such individuals as Kurosawa's couple on a Sunday date with no money in *One Wonderful Sunday*, or the happier boy and girl in Shiro Toyoda's section (after a Kurosawa script) of *Four Love Stories*. One of the attributes of individuality is perspective, and so a few films began to laugh at the brave new world which was being created: an example was Yoshimura's *The Fellows Who Ate the Elephant*, about five hungry men who consume the zoo's elephant and get into an enormous amount of difficulty with bureaucratic authorities. More subtly critical was Ozu's *The Record of a Tenement Gentleman*, about one of the boys who roamed the streets after the war. He eventually meets his father, but rejects him and goes off to make his own life, an ambivalent comment on the passing of the family and the need of the young for a new way.

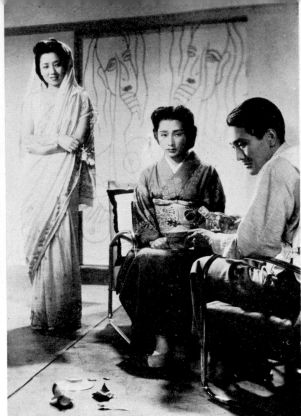

LEFT: *A Ball at the Anjo House*, 1947, directed by Kozaburo Yoshimura, with (from left) Yumeko Aizome, Masayuki Mori, Osamu Takizawa, and Setsuko Hara. RIGHT: *Once More*, 1947, directed by Heinosuke Gosho, with (from left) Yuriko Hamada, Mieko Takamine, and Haruo Tanaka.

ANOTHER poignant glance at the passing of the old was Yoshimura's *A Ball at the Anjo House*, a movie about the final party held in one of the last mansions. During it we examine the memories of the family, of the servants; we see the young people, already strangers to their tradition. What these young folk would do was suggested in Gosho's *Once More*, a film about changes in Japanese intellectual life and the search for something to believe in.

To the End of the Silver-capped Mountains, 1947, directed by Senkichi Taniguchi. ABOVE: Takashi Shimura. ABOVE RIGHT: Toshiro Mifune. RIGHT: *War And Peace*, 1947, directed by Satsuo Yamamoto and Fumio Kamei.

WHAT THE generation faced was shown quite graphically in *War and Peace* (no relation to Tolstoy) of Satsuo Yamamoto and Fumio Kamei, about two soldiers returning from the war and meeting with indifference and poverty. To a people without any kind of security, a call to some kind of political social action was most attractive, and for a time (particularly after the Occupation ended) Communist-line films filled the theaters. But people are people, and what eventually began filling theaters was a new kind of film which said that not worrying about problems is one way of treating them. The answer was entertainment, particularly "melodrama," a genre which to the Japanese means at least some amount of violence. One of the first and most successful was the cops-and-robbers thriller, *To the End of the Silver-capped Mountains*. About a gang of bank-robbers who try to escape into the Japan Alps, the picture was made almost entirely on location and was among the first to continue the tradition of realism in Japanese film. It also marked the debut of an actor later to become world famous: Toshiro Mifune.

83

LEFT: *Apostasy*, 1948, directed by Keisuke Kinoshita, with Ryo Ikebe (left) and Yoko Katsuragi. BELOW: scenes from *Drunken Angel*, 1948, directed by Akira Kurosawa. LEFT: Michiyo Kogure (left) and Toshiro Mifune (right). RIGHT: Mifune and Takashi Shimura.

MIFUNE was also the star of Kurosawa's *Drunken Angel*, a picture which has come to mean postwar Japan as much as *Paisa* has come to stand for postwar Italy. Set in the ruins of Tokyo around a sump which, as the film progresses, comes to symbolize the rotten center of a profiteering, new-rich, hoodlum-ridden society, the picture explores with the greatest delicacy and strength the relations between an alcoholic doctor who feels he must save someone and a tubercular gangster who, unwillingly, needs to be saved. This lifting of the lid from a contemporary evil, and doing so in the form of an exciting, action-filled "melodrama," both shocked and thrilled the audience. It was also one of the first films which criticized the present rather than the past. There were soon others. Even today most Japanese will deny the existence of an actively discriminated against pariah caste. There is just such a caste, however, and Kinoshita's *Apostasy* showed it.

TOP LEFT: *Women of the Night*, 1948, directed by Kenji Mizoguchi, with Kumeko Urabe (left) and Kinuyo Tanaka. RIGHT: *A Hen in the Wind*, 1948, directed by Yasujiro Ozu, with Shuji Sano (left) and Kinuyo Tanaka. CENTER LEFT: *The Chess King*, 1948, directed by Daisuke Ito with Tsumasaburo Bando (right). RIGHT: *The Day Our Lives Shine*, 1948, directed by Kozaburo Yoshimura, with Masayuki Mori (left) and Yoshiko Yamaguchi.

THE LOT OF the prostitute had either been falsified or ignored. In *Women of the Night*, Mizoguchi turned his attention to fallen women and their actual lives. His findings so shocked the nation that this picture (along with his last film, *Red-Light District*) was instrumental in having the anti-prostitution law passed in Japan. Even Ozu treated the subject in *A Hen in the Wind*, in which a husband comes to understand how his wife was forced into prostitution during the war because of poverty. Though Daisuke Ito was usually making period pictures, he turned to the contemporary-life picture to make *The Chess King*, one of the first of the postwar films to complain about gangsters. Films were becoming very critical indeed, and in *The Day Our Lives Shine*, Yoshimura even seemed to attack the Occupation on the grounds that Japan was becoming a "dollar colony." Touchy Occupation officials reprimanded him for this, and some of the film was cut.

85

LEFT: *Children of the Beehive*, 1948, directed by Hiroshi Shimizu. BELOW RIGHT: shooting the film, director Shimizu in middle. BELOW LEFT: *Children Hand in Hand*, 1948, directed by Hiroshi Inagaki.

ANOTHER social ill that much deserved attention was the plight of the many homeless, parentless children after the war. In *Children of the Beehive*, Hiroshi Shimizu made a film about the gangs of boys which wandered the streets and parks; in *Children Hand in Hand*, Hiroshi Inagaki suggested ways in which they could be schooled and taught.

TOP: *Blue Mountains*, 1948, directed by Tadashi Imai, with Ryo Ikebe (left) and Yoko Sugi. CENTER *The Broken Drum*, 1949, directed by Keisuke Kinoshita, with Tsumasaburo Bando (left) and Masayuki Mori. BOTTOM: *Here's to the Girls*, 1949, directed by Keisuke Kinoshita, with Shuji Sano (left).

THAT CHILDREN should be helped to find their way in the new world but should also be allowed to make their own decisions was the burden of Imai's very popular *Blue Mountains*, about teen-age love and parental authority. Kinoshita was also taking a dim view of the elders. The title of one of his films, *The Broken Drum*, referred to the father (the last film-role of Tsumasaburo Bando) and showed his futile attempts to rule his family with feudal precepts. Another, *Here's to the Girls*, had much the same message. A young working man loves a girl from the aristocracy. She loves him too, and all the machinations of both their parents cannot keep them apart.

TOP LEFT: *Quiet Duel*, 1949, directed by Akira Kuro-
sawa, with Noriko Sengoku (left) and Toshiro Mifune.
RIGHT: scenes from *Stray Dog*, 1949, directed by Akira
Kurosawa, with Toshiro Mifune.

THE PHILOSOPHY of the times was that one must make one's own decisions,
and this became one of Kurosawa's major themes. In *Quiet Duel*, he has his
innocently syphilitic doctor (he got it while operating) decide to turn his
back on his long-suffering girl friend and devote himself to medicine. In a
much better picture, *Stray Dog*, Kurosawa presented a full-scale picture of
Tokyo society (the hero chases his stolen pistol through all the lower strata
of the city), and at the same time said very plainly that though you must
make your own decisions, you must at the same time bear the consequences
of your actions—such as having a pistol stolen and then used to murder—
because this too is your own fault.

TOP: *A Women's Life*, 1949, directed by Fumio Kamei, with Nobuko Otowa. BOTTOM: scenes from *Late Spring*, 1949, directed by Yasujiro Ozu. LEFT: Setsuko Hara (left) and Chishu Ryu. RIGHT: Ozu directing a scene.

AT THE SAME time—in Japan more than in most countries—there is a corresponding temptation not to act at all rather than take responsibility for one's actions. With failure presumed assured, it is easier not to try. This accounts for the high suicide rate, on one hand, and some extraordinary films on the other. Not taking responsibilities, not trying, need not be the craven thing most Westerners believe it to be. Accepting life as it is can also be a way of transcendence. Ozu, Naruse, and to some extent Mizoguchi, have celebrated this quality. Kurosawa, on the other hand, has made it the only villain to be found in his films. Usually social pressures are shown as responsible for this quietism: Fumio Kamei's *A Woman's Life* (a hardy perennial based on the Maupassant) showed the world as simply too much for a single woman. Yoshimura's debunking of a feudal hero in *Ishimatsu from Mori* had the swordsman getting around the problem by cynically taking no

89

responsibility for anything, relegating it to others, and then taking the credit. Ozu, in *Late Spring* and other of his later films, however, defines the truly Japanese way—to the extent that he was called "the most Japanese of all Japanese directors"—which is to observe the unfriendly world, to recognize one's own limits and live in harmony both with the self and the world by refusing to trespass, by refusing conflict, by accepting the chaos and injustice, by realizing that all things pass and that the self changes just as much as the world does. In this film, the father and daughter have lived together for years. Now the daughter must marry. They go to Kyoto on a final trip together, and then he is left alone—a favorite Ozu image, the parent alone at the end. He is sad but not lonely. His inner strength, his acceptance of the world and of his own emotions have prepared him. He sits alone in the house and slowly peels an apple. His hands busy, he looks ahead, tranquil, and this beautiful picture ends.

CENTER: *Late Spring*, with (from left) Chishu Ryu, Haruko Sugimura and Setsuko Hara. LEFT: *Ishimatsu from Mori*, 1949, directed by Kozaburo Yoshimura, with Yukiko Todoroki (left) and Susumu Fujita.

Rashomon, 1950, directed by Akira Kurosawa. TOP: (from left) Toshiro Mifune, Masayuki Mori and Machiko Kyo. CENTER LEFT: (from left) Minoru Chiaki, Kichijiro Ueda and Takashi Shimura. RIGHT: Mifune and Kyo.

THIS QUALITY has a name. It is called *mono no awaré*, and it implies a recognition, indeed even a satisfaction, in the natural mutation, the natural evanescence of our lives. In Ozu's *Munekata Sisters*, the disappointed sister is not unhappy; she is content and from this acceptance finds strength. In Mizoguchi, as in Ozu, strength comes not from acting but from accepting the inevitable. *The Picture of Madame Yuki* is partially a tragedy because the heroine cannot accept the inevitable, because she insists upon doing things in order to keep her lovers, in order to keep from growing old. *Mono no awaré* would insist that upon looking at the mirror in the morning and observing one more wrinkle, the reaction would be: Well, good, all is well with the

91

world—things are going as they ought. Its opposite would be an emotion like that in Dylan Thomas': "Do not go gentle into that good night...rage, rage against the dying of the light." Its opposite is also found in that famous film *Rashomon*, where Kurosawa refuses to accept the nature of visible truth and the nature of visible reality. Since the movies can only show us this superficial and visible reality, one of the many fascinations of this film is that we are shown the palpably real and are told it is false. Another is that, with its varied recounting of different eye-witness retellings of a rape and a murder, the film states that nothing is real, that everything is interpretation. It constituted an extremely strong protest against things as they seem.

The Munakata Sisters, 1950, directed by Yasujiro Ozu. ABOVE LEFT: Ozu rehearsing with Hisako Yamane (left) and Hideko Takamine. RIGHT: the two actresses in a scene. LEFT: *The Picture of Madam Yuki*, 1950, directed by Kenji Mizoguchi, with Michiyo Kogure (left) and Yoshiko Kuga.

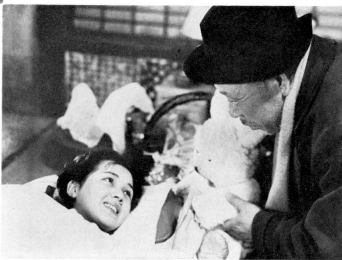

TOP: *Conduct Report of Professor Ishinaka*, 1950, directed by Mikio Naruse, with (from left) Yoko Sugi, Kamatari Fujiwara, Ryo Ikebe, and Zeko Nakamura. CENTER: *Scandal*, 1950, directed by Akira Kurosawa, with Yoko Katsuragi (left) and Takashi Shimura. LEFT: *Until the Day We Meet Again*, 1950, directed by Tadashi Imai, with Eiji Okada (left) and Yoshiko Kuga.

RASHOMON was but one—though by far the best—of the varied protests of the period which was just now, after the shock of war and occupation, beginning to find its voice. It protested against the entire human condition, while the same director's *Scandal*, filmed in the same year, protested against the intrusion of the press and the postwar scandal-mongering of the yellow press which, in the new freedom after the war, habitually confused liberty with license. Naruse's *Conduct Report of Professor Ishinaka* was about the same thing, people thrusting their noses into other people's business. In *Until The Day We Meet Again*, Tadashi Imai again raged against the war and the military but this time showed its effect on two wartime lovers. In *And Yet We Live*, his protest became more explicit and insisted upon political action and social change. Equally reformatory and polemical in its intent was Hideo Sekigawa's *Listen to the Roar of the Ocean*, the "ocean" of the title being the common man aroused.

93

TOP: *Listen to the Roar of the Ocean*, 1950 directed by
Hideo Sekigawa. ABOVE LEFT: *And Yet We Live*, 1951, di-
rected by Tadashi Imai; Imai directing a scene.
RIGHT: Shizue (left) and Chojuro Kawarazaki.

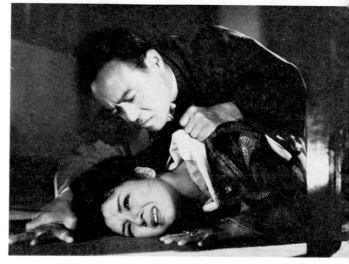

TOP: *The Idiot*, 1951, directed by Akira Kurosawa, with Toshiro Mifune (left) and Masayuki Mori. ABOVE: (from left) Kurosawa, Takashi Shimura, Setsuko Hara, Yoshiko Kuga, Mori, and Mifune. ABOVE RIGHT: *Carmen Comes Home*, 1951, directed by Keisuke Kinoshita, with Hideko Takamine (left) and Toshiko Kobayashi. RIGHT: *Clothes of Deception*, 1951, directed by Kozaburo Yoshimura, with Machiko Kyo (below) and Ichiro Sugai.

GIVEN A COMMON acceptance of *mono no awaré*, an aroused Japanese populace is unlikely. Besides, protesting a political system and protesting against the human condition are two different things, and herein lie the differences between directors like Sekigawa and Imai, and a director like Kurosawa. In *The Idiot*, the latter (through Dostoevsky) tackled one of life's central problems: how to be yourself, that is, realize your own potentialities, and at the same time do so at the least expense of others; or, put the other way, how do you exercise compassion, which is the most human of all emotions, and at the same time realize yourself? This problem is as central to Kurosawa's pictures as it is to life, particularly over-crowded, competitive, but still Buddhist-influenced Japanese life. In Japan the problem is dramatized in the dilemma of the woman. She finds herself (even after the war) in a condition which insists that she become slowly invisible, a combination

95

book and baby-machine. Her problem is how to realize herself as a person and at the same time avoid forfeiting a place in a society which frowns upon this realization. *Carmen Comes Home* of Kinoshita and *Clothes of Deception* of Yoshimura were both about the problem, though the first is a very funny comedy (a self-made woman, a strip-tease artist, visits the scenes of her childhood), and the second is a tragedy (about a geisha who loses all in trying to become a person). In Naruse's *Repast*, the wife begins to realize that all these years with the same man have given her neither self-respect nor self-realization. Ozu's *Early Summer* was about the same thing: the break-up of a marriage, the break-up of a family. Marital and personal problems were also seen in an exceptional historical picture, Yoshimura's *A Tale from Genji*, the first film version of the first novel, the twelfth-century *Genji Monogatari*.

LEFT: *Repast*, 1951, directed by Mikio Naruse, with Setsuko Hara (left) and Ken Uehara. BOTTOM LEFT: *Early Summer*, 1951, directed by Yasujiro Ozu, with (from left) Kuniko Miyake, Kan Nihonyanaʒi and Setsuko Hara. RIGHT: *A Tale f Genji*, 1951, directed by Kozaburo Yoshimura, with Kazuo Hasegawa (left) and Michiyo Kogure.

TOP: *The Life of Oharu*, 1952, directed by Kenji Mizoguchi, with Kinuyo Tanaka. *Carmen's Pure Love*, 1952, directed by Keisuke Kinoshita. CENTER LEFT: Chikage Awashima (left) and Eiko Miyoshi. RIGHT: Toshiko Kobayashi (left) and Hideko Takamine.

As IN THE historical pictures of Kenji Mizoguchi, the emphasis in *A Tale from Genji* was upon the reality of the heroine's plight, as real in the twelfth century as in the twentieth. In *The Life of Oharu*, Mizoguchi illustrated the same theme with a prodigality of beauty and detail which made these last historical films of the director a near-miraculous combination of the humanly meaningful and the completely beautiful. This film version of a novel by the eighteenth-century writer Saikaku chronicled the decline of a court lady who ends a prostitute. Few who have seen it will ever forget the sad beauty of its final scenes where Oharu, now an old woman, slowly walks through a temple compound, remembering her life as the sun sets behind her. That the hardness of woman's lot is also somewhat her own fault was the theme of Kinoshita's satire, *Carmen's Pure Love*. Here the heroine decides that if anything is to be done she must do it herself, and, like Candide on his travels, she at once runs up against the idiocy of the modern world while Kinoshita makes fun of everything from planned motherhood to the atom bomb.

97

TOP: *Mother*, 1952, directed by Mikio Naruse, with Kyoko Kagawa (left) and Eiji Okada. *The Taste of Green Tea And Rice*, 1952, directed by Yasujiro Ozu. CENTER: Ozu directing a scene. BOTTOM: (from left) Keiko Tsushima, Shin Saburi, and Koji Tsuruta.

IN *Mother*, Naruse celebrated the very ties that bind, making a warm comedy out of the social and economic difficulties of belonging to the lower-middle classes. One of the most successful of these postwar *shomin-geki*, it shared with Ozu's *The Taste of Green Tea and Rice* a concern for human feelings and aspirations which it found beautiful, at the same time admitting that the feeling would not remain and that the aspirations were never to be realized.

98

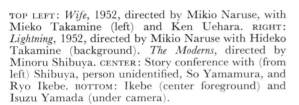

TOP LEFT: *Wife*, 1952, directed by Mikio Naruse, with Mieko Takamine (left) and Ken Uehara. RIGHT: *Lightning*, 1952, directed by Mikio Naruse with Hideko Takamine (background). *The Moderns*, directed by Minoru Shibuya. CENTER: Story conference with (from left) Shibuya, person unidentified, So Yamamura, and Ryo Ikebe. BOTTOM: Ikebe (center foreground) and Isuzu Yamada (under camera).

IN BOTH *Wife* and *Lightning*, Naruse's view of the middle-class family was less reassuring. In both, the woman realizes that life should be more than working and being unhappy. In both, as in so many of the later Naruse films, she decides to do something about it. She does—and she runs directly into that stone wall which, says Naruse, exists between Japanese and, by extension, between everyone. That this need not be tragic is suggested by two of Minoru Shibuya's early pictures. *The Moderns* is a wry comedy about young people trying to live without such traditional restraints, and failing. *No Consultation Today* is a very funny film about a doctor who is determined that there must be a way to help even the awfullest people. His encounter with the stone wall (as real to Shibuya as it is to Naruse) accounts for most of the comedy.

99

LEFT: *No Consultation Today*, 1952, directed by Minoru Shibuya, with (from left) Chikage Awashima, Koji Tsuruta and Eijiro Yanagi. BELOW: *Ikiru*, 1952, directed by Akira Kurosawa, with Takashi Shimura.

WHAT THEN to do about life? This is the question which more and more Japanese films were asking during this sober period when the war was becoming history and the term "postwar" could no longer be used as an excuse for not doing anything. One answer was given in one of Japan's finest films, Akira Kurosawa's *Ikiru*. His petty official, dying of cancer and terrified both of death and also of the life he has failed to either realize or redeem, flings himself first into pleasure, then into companionship. Both failing, he turns to work, and in the very teeth of official indifference, forces through a park for children. Kurosawa says that life has precisely the meaning that you choose to give it, neither more nor less. This near existential thesis is also Japanese; it shares much with Zen and, particularly, with Indian Buddhism. Certainly, it appears the opposite of *mono no awaré*, and yet both ways include a final acceptance of self and a final acceptance of responsibility.

100

LEFT: scene from *Ikiru*, with Yunosuke Ito (left) and Takashi Shimura. CENTER LEFT: Akira Kurosawa and Shimura. RIGHT: *Children of the Atom Bomb*, 1952, directed by Kaneto Shindo, with Nobuko Otowa.

A THESIS as stringent, as hard-boiled as this will never be popular because, for any people, it is much more comforting to believe that you are what you are made to be. The corollary that what you make of what has been made of you is the more important—this falls on ears as deaf in Japan as elsewhere. The Japanese, for example, continued for years to find excuses in the admittedly inhuman atrocity of the atom-bombing of Hiroshima and Nagasaki. Kaneto Shindo's very moving *Children of the Atom Bomb* suggested that something now be done for those young lives already shaped and ruined. This picture was greeted with indignation by its sponsors, the Japan Teachers' Union, because Shindo had "destroyed the story's political orientation." They commissioned another film.

101

THIS WAS Hideo Sekigawa's *Hiroshima*, a picture which fulfilled all expectations because it stated so plainly that Americans had ruined everything and that the only thing that the Japanese could do was to sit and mourn. This picture was widely shown in America (and parts of it also appeared in Resnais' *Hiroshima, mon amour*), where the audience, quite rightly afflicted with a bad conscience, failed to see that pointing a deserved accusing finger was not the only way of coping with the hideous fact of the bombings of the cities and the needless massacre of their inhabitants. Sekigawa and others continued to grind political axes with this and other atom-bomb pictures. That leftist films need not be morally suspect simply because they are leftist was indicated in So Yamamura's brilliant *Crab-canning Boat*, where a notorious example of completely capitalistic exploitation was exposed, criticized, and rectified.

ABOVE: *Hiroshima*, 1953, directed by Hideo Sekigawa, with Nobuko Otowa (lying). RIGHT: *Crab-canning Boat*, 1953. So Yamamura (center) directing.

102

TOP: Scene from *The Tower of Lilies*, 1953, directed by Tadashi Imai, with Keiko Tsushima and Kyoko Kagawa. CENTER LEFT: *Eagle of the Pacific*, 1953, directed by Inoshiro Honda, with Denjiro Okochi (left). RIGHT: *The Thick-walled Room*, 1953, directed by Masaki Kobayashi.

A MORE HONEST re-examination of the horrors of war was Imai's *The Tower of Lilies*, about the fate of a number of Okinawan schoolgirls during the taking of the island. Though Imai allowed himself a number of melodramatics, he was in this and other films much more interested in the way people act than in the way they ought to. The American tanks warn that the cave in which the girls are sheltering will be bombarded and that anyone inside should come out. The girls refuse, the cave is bombed, all the girls die, and the inference is that, people being people, neither side could have acted any differently. Other war films, such as *Eagle of the Pacific*, led a long line (still continuing) insisting that war is somehow heroic. Still others, like Kobayashi's *The Thick-walled Room*, was about the vexed question of "war guilt" and the right of the Allied Tribunal to try and condemn men who were, after all, only doing their duty. *Red-Light Bases* openly and honestly pointed out that these same victors were now responsible for at least a part of the postwar corruption of the country. At the same time, this film (unlike others which later shared a similar theme) was equally hard on the vanquished for being so completely corruptible.

LEFT: *Red-light Bases*, 1953, directed by Senkichi Taniguchi, with Akemi Negishi (left). BELOW: *Muddy Waters*, 1953, directed by Tadashi Imai, with Chikage Awashima (foreground).

104

LEFT: *Before Dawn*, 1953, directed by Kozaburo Yoshi-
mura, with Nobuko Otowa. BELOW LEFT AND CENTER:
Where Chimneys Are Seen, 1953, directed by Heinosuke
Gosho, with Kinuyo Tanaka and Ken Uehara. RIGHT:
A Japanese Tragedy, 1954, directed by Keisuke Kino-
shita.

 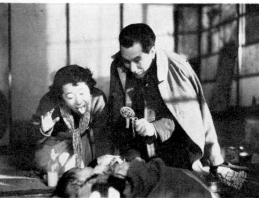 

THE ATTITUDE of the Japanese toward themselves shares that of many other
peoples, but there are differences. One can detect an almost Teutonic in-
sistence that people are what they are made, and that social conditions make
or break—usually the latter. At the same time, and completely unlike the
Germans, the Japanese have a passion for living, a passion for nature which
is comparable to that of the Greeks or the Italians. Living, as seen in the
films of Naruse, or Gosho, or Ozu, is a sweet thing, despite the almost over-
whelming economic and emotional problems. This combination of shifting
the blame onto outside conditions and, at the same time, celebrating the
very results of these conditions makes the Japanese attitude toward themselves a peculiarly rich one. It saves from over-simplification, for example,
those social-protest films so threadbare in other counties. Imai's *Muddy
Waters* is about the hard and dreary lot of women, and there is an implicit
call for reaction, if not revolution. Yet, at the same time, Imai shows the
beauty of these uneventful lives where, if there are no great heights, neither
are there great depths. In Yoshimura's *Before Dawn* and Gosho's *Where
Chimneys Are Seen*, more important than a criticism of whatever it is that keeps
the lower-middle classes low is an appreciation of the continual will to do
better which animates these people's lives. One of the characters in the latter
film tries to balance a pencil on its end and after many failures succeeds.
His pleasure at this simple feat is important, and Gosho shows it as that. Even
when a film sets out to show the hopelessness of being Japanese, as does
Kinoshita's *A Japanese Tragedy*, it also shows that life continues, that existence
is endless, that sorrow heals itself, and that even suicide (the mother kills
herself at the end of the picture) is but an incident in an eternal flow.

105

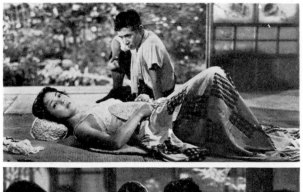

TOP LEFT: *Older Brother, Young Sister*, 1953, directed by Kozaburo Yoshimura, with Machiko Kyo and Masayuki Mori. CENTER: *A Thousand Cranes*, 1953, directed by Kozaburo Yoshimura, with Nobuko Otowa (second from left) and Michiyo Kogure (center). *Wild Geese*, 1953, directed by Shiro Toyoda.

LEFT BOTTOM: Toyoda (center) with Hideko Takamine (left) and Eijiro Tono. TOP RIGHT: Hiroshi Akutagawa (left) and Hideko Takamine. CENTER RIGHT: *What's Your Name?* 1953, directed by Hideo Ohba, with Mie Kitahara (above) and Keiji Sada.

THIS ATTITUDE seems peculiarly Japanese (or, better, peculiarly Asian), this tension between the need for action, social or personal, and the observation that life is life and that doomed action (or no action at all) becomes beautiful because it is so plainly natural. Thus Japanese films are full of incomplete, tentative attempts at a better life. The attempt fails, and just there lies its beauty, just as the beauty of the cherry blossoms is said to be not when they are in full bloom but when they begin to fall. Yoshimura's *Older Brother, Younger Sister* shows a girl rebelling and then succumbing; *A Thousand Cranes* shows a wife turning away from her husband and then turning back. Toyoda's beautiful *Wild Geese* is about a girl who is a kept mistress and whose love turns toward a young student about to leave Japan for study abroad. He is unaware of her feelings; even she is only partially aware of them. She does not know the extent of her need, and it is without bitterness that she returns to her keeper. Even such popular entertainment as *What's Your Name* (one of the world's longest films, running over eight hours when all of its parts are shown together) insists that the two lovers' failing (by inches) to meet is right, proper, and beautiful.

106

Tokyo Story, 1953, directed by Yasujiro Ozu. TOP LEFT: Chishu Ryu and Chieko Higashiyama. TOP RIGHT: (from left) So Yamamura, Setsuko Hara, Haruko Sugimura, Kyoko Kagawa, and Higashiyama. RIGHT: (from left) Sugimura, Ryu, Yamamura, Shiro Osaka, Hara, and Kagawa.

THIS, THEN, is *mono no awaré,* a term for which the West has no equivalent unless it is *lacrimae rerum,* the pathos of things. This connection is between sadness (not only the transcience of earthly things, but also the brute facts of social or political oppression) and beauty. The beautiful (a river, a death, a tree, a first love) is eternal in that it lives and dies, this cycle occurring over and over again. It is therefore possible to view even labor-union troubles as a part of the eternal flux. This completely traditional way of looking at life is responsible for a national philosophy of "it can't be helped" and, at the same time, is equally responsible for a celebration of the small things of life which may end up in the apotheosis of the tea ceremony (table manners removed to the level of rite), or a very plain and pretty way of coping with that most notorious of social problems, the way to say goodbye and take leave. Yasujiro Ozu in all of his later films captured this essential but elusive quality in Japanese life, and perhaps nowhere did he so completely show this beauty than in *Tokyo Story.* An old couple comes to the city to see their preoccupied children. Back home, the mother dies, and it is now the children who visit the southern town where they were born. It is only the daughter-in-law, not really a member of this typically far-flung family, who understands the feelings of the father. She suggests that she stay with him now that he is alone. Alone, however, is what life has made him, and he prefers it thus. This extraordinary acceptance of life is what the director— using one of the most marvelously elliptical techniques in all cinema—shows, and by showing, blesses.

107

TOP LEFT: *Gion Music*, 1953, directed by Kenji Mizoguchi, with Kikue Mori and Ayako Wakao (facing each other). RIGHT: *The Gate of Hell*, 1953, directed by Teinosuke Kinugasa, with Machiko Kyo (left) and Kazuo Hasegawa. CENTER LEFT AND BOTTOM RIGHT: *Ugetsu*, 1953, directed by Kenji Mizoguchi, with Machiko Kyo and Masayuki Mori.

108

MIZOGUCHI in his later years came to share this philosophy. The geisha in *Gion Music* finally settle for what life can give them. The potter in that fabulous allegory of the human spirit, *Ugetsu*, leaves his wife to live with the dead. After a period with the beautiful spirit, he returns to find that his wife—who meets him, feeds him—is also dead. He finds that the world of the spirit was always with him, waiting for him to return. To gain this knowledge, however, he must lose both wife and mistress. In the terms of the Japanese ethos (as shown in the kabuki, for example) he experiences the impossibility of combining duty (wife) and inclination (mistress); in terms of *mono no awaré* he has acted and now he must accept that these actions brought him no nearer satisfaction, but that (more important) he has come to realize a larger pattern, a pattern in which he too has his small part. The next morning he and his son begin their new life together. There are also words for the peculiar and plain beauty to be found in the celebration of the natural, or the inevitable. One of these is *shibui*, an esthetic term which might be used to describe the quietly elegant, almost carefully unostentatious final films of Mizoguchi. A further meaning of the word is that this elegance is slightly bitter, as a lemon is bitter. This astringency is refreshing. The opposite term, *hadé* (the difference between a full Chinese banquet and the taste of green tea over rice) might be applied to that popular color film, *The Gate of Hell*, in which Kinugasa constructed a phantasmagora in which kitsch was pushed to a height very near art. *Hadé* is loud without being vulgar, highly decorated without being merely busy, noisy without being rude, and in this picture, Kinugasa exhibited quite another aspect of the also completely Japanese way.

Scene from *Ugetsu*.

TOP LEFT: *Return of Godzilla*, 1955, directed by Moto-
yoshi Oda. RIGHT: *Radon*, 1956, directed by Ichiro
Honda. CENTER LEFT: *King Kong vs. Godzilla*, 1962, directed by Ichiro Honda. RIGHT: *Mothra vs. Godzilla*,
1964, directed by Ichiro Honda.

HADÉ INDEED were the spate of monster and science-fiction films which have
probably accounted for more foreign viewings of Japanese film than *Rashomon*, *Ugetsu*, and *Gate of Hell* put together. Regardless of the monster involved,
the story is always the same. It is always about how Japan (the "new Swit-
zerland") saves the world from total war or monster-invasion by intervening
at the proper time. The monsters or the visitors from outer space usually
choose Japan because (thanks to the atom-bomb) Japan knows more about
wholesale destruction than anywhere else. But the choice, from the monster's
point of view, is never too happy because there are always at least several
Japanese scientists who are more than ready to lay down their lives to ensure
its demise. Not that they do their job any too well: Godzilla is eaten away
by a new chemical placed at his feet by doomed scientists, but in *The Return
of Godzilla* he is up and about again, this time descending from the frozen
North. In *Godzilla Versus King Kong*, he is again ambulatory and this time
becomes friendly enough to join Radon and Mothra in combatting yet a
new monster. The more familiar the monster the less dangerous he is—the
Japanese like the known. By the time they have appeared in several films
they are already old friends, and (in true *mono no awaré* fashion) we are
invited to feel for them when they too must be destroyed. It is not surprising
that the Japanese should make so many trick-films and do them so well. They
took to the films of Méliès as did few other nations, and the first Western
author to be translated in this country was Jules Verne.

110

Twenty-four Eyes, 1954, directed by Keisuke Kinoshita. ABOVE: Kinoshita with Zenzo Matsuyama (kneeling). RIGHT: Hideko Takamine (left).

ONE OF THE reasons that the monster-pix should be so popular is not only that they are exciting, *hadé,* and comfortingly moral, but also that they are so realistic. The Japanese concern for reality is, as we have seen, extreme. It is so real that it can even be questioned in a film like *Rashomon.* One occasionally hears that Japanese movies (particularly scenes of city-life) look stagey. If they do it is because Japanese cities themselves look quite stagey. The average downtown street with its neon and plastic does indeed look like a movie set. One always expects flaps and braces upon rounding a corner. This also the Japanese film reflects with the most scrupulous exactitude. One of the reasons that the Japanese film continues to look so real is that real locations are so often used. Part of the reason for this is financial, and part of it is the lack of really enormous studio facilities. Most of it, however, is the assumption—an assumption found in all the Japanese arts—that the natural, things as they are, are the things to show, the things to talk about. *Twenty-four Eyes* is a fine example. This Kinoshita film was shot almost entirely on location (the island of Shodoshima in the Inland Sea) and is about the life of a girl who becomes a school teacher, who loses her husband and son in the war, and who is remembered by her pupils. In films like this and those of Gosho, Toyoda, Ozu, and Naruse during this period, Japan produced films of a directness and an honesty, a freedom from tight plot and contrived story, which reflected life with a fidelity rare on the screen.

111

TOP: *The Garden of Women*, 1954, directed by Keisuke Kinoshita, with Hideko Takamine (left) and Takahiro Tamura. *An Inn in Osaka*, 1954, directed by Heinosuke Gosho. CENTER LEFT: (from left) Shuji Sano, Nobuko Otowa, and Gosho. RIGHT: Otowa and Sano.

ONE SUCH picture was Kinoshita's *The Garden of Women*, and another was Gosho's splendid *An Inn in Osaka*. This latter, one of the finest of all *shomingeki*, was about a small Japanese-style hotel and the lives of those who worked and lived there. Everything is incident and character and the calm, very Japanese assurance that things are so bad now that they can only become better.

TOP LEFT: *That Woman*, 1954, directed by Shiro Toyoda, with Machiko Kyo. TOP RIGHT: *Sounds from the Mountain*, 1954, directed by Mikio Naruse, with (from left) Setsuko Hara, Teruko Nagaoka, and So Yamamura; CENTER: *The Story of Shunkin*, 1954, directed by Daisuke Ito, with Yoshiaki Hanayagi (left) and Machiko Kyo; BOTTOM: *The Sound of Waves*, 1954, directed by Senkichi Taniguchi, with Akira Kubo (left) and Kyoko Aoyama.

THIS FEELING is so very akin to that in Japanese literature that it is not surprising that there are so many excellent literary adaptations. Among these are Toyoda's *That Woman* and Naruse's *Sounds from the Mountains*. Tanizaki's novel about the blind *koto* player and her servant-lover was remade in Daisuke Ito's *The Story of Shunkin,* and Senkichi Taniguchi made Mishima's reworking of Daphnis and Chloe into a charming picture called *The Sound of Waves.*

113

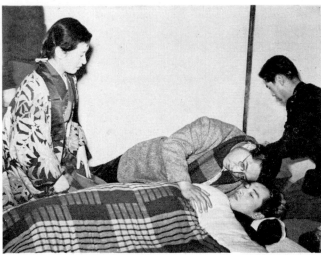

TOP LEFT: *Cape Ashizuri*, 1954, directed by Kozaburo shima. RIGHT: Yoshimura (center) and the two actors. CENTER LEFT: *Musashi Miyamoto*, 1954, directed by Hiroshi Inagaki, with Kaoru Yachigusa (left) and Toshiro Mifune. RIGHT: Inagaki and Mifune (foreground).

ANOTHER such adaptation was Yoshimura's version of *Cape Ashizuri*, and Inagaki made into a film one of the great historical best sellers, *Musashi Miyamoto*, with Toshiro Mifune, which went on to win the 1954 Academy Award, though in a much cut version. It was necessary to cut it because, in a way, this was very much like one of the "new" period films of the 1930's. Since everyone knew the story already, Inagaki would often leave out sections of the continuity and would cut away to such natural illustrations as a mountain torrent to indicate passion, a falling cherry petal representing transcience. These by 1954 were all clichés, but the cliché is peculiarly potent with the Japanese public.

LEFT: *Sansho the Bailiff*, 1954, directed by Kenji Mizoguchi, with Kinuyo Tanaka (left) and Chieko Naniwa (second from right). BELOW: *A Story from Chikamatsu*, 1954, directed by Kenji Mizoguchi, with Kyoko Kagawa (left) and Kazuo Hasegawa.

INFINITELY more original and much more powerful were two Mizoguchi period films. *Sansho the Bailiff* is the story of two children separated from their mother during the thirteenth-century period of civil wars. Finally, at the end of the mother's life, the son finds her again. *A Story from Chikamatsu* was taken from one of the kabuki plays of that eighteenth-century playwright. In it, a rich merchant's wife is suspected by her husband of infidelity with an apprentice. It is just this suspicion which drives her to the apprentice— and to their destruction. While both of these films were meticulously realistic historical reconstructions, the psychology of the people was completely contemporary, as Japan still contained high-level tyrants like Sansho and a number of jealous husbands.

Scenes from *Seven Samurai*, 1954, directed by Akira
Kurosawa. TOP: (from left) Takashi Shimura, Ko
Kimura, and Toshiro Mifune.

THE GREATEST of all Japanese period films and perhaps the finest Japanese
film ever made was Kurosawa's *Seven Samurai*. It was about a group of poor
farmers who asked seven masterless samurai (*rōnin*) to protect their village
from bandits. During the film the seven save the village, though three of
their number are killed. At the end the farmers, forgetting the samurai, go
on with their lives, and the remaining three realize that friendship, winning
a war, even love, mean little; and that the round of the seasons, rice-planting,
rice-harvesting, are the only verities. This is what the leader of the samurai
means when he says: "Again we survive—and again we lose. The winners
are the farmers, not us."

116

Scenes from *Seven Samurai*. TOP RIGHT: Kurosawa (right) with Mifune. CENTER: Mifune (foreground) in a scene. BOTTOM: (from left) Takashi Shimura, Daisuke Kato and Ko Kimura.

117

TOP: *The Beauty and the Dragon*, 1955, directed by Kozaburo Yoshimura, with Nobuko Otowa (left) and Chiyonosuke Azuma. RIGHT: *A Bloody Spear at Mount Fuji*, 1955, directed by Tomu Uchida, with Chiezo Kataoka (standing).

THE SAMURAI are modern men, and what they experience is what we all experience. One of the great strengths of the Kurosawa film was that the experience, the reduction of action to its meaning, was so personal, honest, and unsentimental. The film refuses to comfort and at the same time shows that even human limitations are—because they are so human—beautiful. Tomu Uchida's *A Bloody Spear at Mount Fuji* and Yoshimura's *The Beauty and the Dragon* also put contemporary psychology in a period setting; indeed, the princess in the latter was a completely modern Tokyo girl who does not believe in bad dragons any more than she believes in love-sick princes. All of the better historical films of the period, including those by Gosho and Toyoda, recognized that the past need not be romanticized.

118

TOP: *Grass-Whistle*, 1955, directed by Shiro Toyoda, with Kyoko Aoyama (left) and Akira Kubo. *Growing Up*, 1955, directed by Heinosuke Gosho. CENTER LEFT: Isuzu Yamada (left) and Hibari Misora (right). RIGHT: Gosho with Yamada (left) and Keiko Kishi.

TOYODA's *Grass-Whistle* was a very tender story of three adolescents, two boys and a girl, each of whom loves the other. Set in the Taisho period, an age fast growing nostalgic to contemporary eyes, the film refused to sentimentalize. Instead, it treated this odd triangle with a concern that showed that one of the realities of Japanese emotional life (adult as well as adolescent) is that love is often killed by fear and ignorance. This was also the theme of Gosho's *Growing Up*. This splendid Meiji-period reconstruction was about a loving little girl who does not realize that, upon becoming nubile, she is destined to be a prostitute.

LEFT: *Marital Relations*, 1955, directed by Shiro Toyoda, with Chikage Awashima (left) and Hisaya Morishige. BELOW: *She Was Like a Wild Chrysanthemum*, 1955, directed by Keisuke Kinoshita, with Shinji Tanaka (left) and Noriko Arita.

ANOTHER Taisho-period film was Toyoda's *Marital Relations*, a very tender yet wry comedy about the love and friendship between a second-class geisha and a completely charming no-good. Of all of the loving reconstructions of the past, however, the best was probably Kinoshita's *She Was Like a Wild Chrysanthemum*, an elegiac film about a man who returns to the scenes of his youth and remembers his first love.

120

TOP LEFT AND RIGHT: shooting of the boat scene, and the scene with Haruko Sugimura (left) in *She Was Like a Wild Chrysanthemum*. CENTER LEFT: *Wolf*, 1955, directed by Kaneto Shindo, with Sanae Takasugi (left) and Nobuko Otowa. BOTTOM: *A Woman's Life*, 1955, directed by Noboru Nakamura, with Chikage Awashima.

THE JAPANESE attitude toward growth, change, and the past is different from that common in the West. There, age and change are often regretted, hence the romanticization of the past. Here, though equally regretted, they are seen as so inevitable that railing against them seems almost pointless. This is a heritage from Japan's history and is found in both the No and the *haiku*; it is also found in most Japanese girls' writing nostalgic diaries and in the it-can't-be-helped national philosophy. Among the many films which share this quality were Hiromichi Horikawa's *The Story of Fast-growing Weeds*, Satsuo Yamamoto's *Duckweed Story*—both of which were about actions in the past determining today—and Shindo Kaneto's *Wolf* and Nakamura's *A Woman's Life*, both of them about a woman who learns to cope with life by accepting it.

Yuzo Kawashima's *Our Town* (no relation to the Wilder play) was about the many lives in the village and the changes which occur within them. *Medals* of Minoru Shibuya was also about a reassessment of the past. An ex-general, remembering days of glory, attempts to make a comeback in the new Self Defense Forces and fails.

Floating Clouds, 1955, directed by Mikio Naruse. TOP LEFT: Naruse (right) rehearsing Hideko Takamine (left) and Masayuki Mori. RIGHT: Takamine and Mori.

THE PERFECT statement of the Japanese attitude toward past and present is found in Mikio Naruse's *Floating Clouds*. During the war, a girl works overseas with the army and takes up with a married man. After the war they meet again in ruined Tokyo and again begin their affair. He—completely Japanese in this respect—is caught among a number of worlds: the prewar and the postwar, his life with his wife and his life with the girl, the past and the present. When she dies, and only then, he discovers what she meant to him. In a chilling and profoundly beautiful final scene, he very carefully puts lipstick on her dead lips—first because she always liked to look young, but second because she somehow looks more alive that way. The audience recognized this hero, the man who disregards the present only to celebrate it when it becomes the past, and responded. It remains one of the best-loved Japanese films ever made.

123

TOP: *The Maid's Kid*, 1955, directed by Tomotaka Tasaka, with Sachiko Hidari.
RIGHT: *Here Is a Spring*, 1955, directed by Tadashi Imai, with Keiko Kishi (left) and Eiji Okada.

THIS REFLECTIVE attitude toward the past is so strong, so natural in novels, in films—even in politics—that there come periods of taking stock, of looking back and comparing. This is what occurred during the years 1950–55 when the Japanese, the Occupation gone and the country once more a national entity, publicly rethought their position and redefined their character. The past is one thing, and the future is another. Equally rich were those many films which now appeared in which the past was forgotten in face of the promise and the danger of the future. One of the nicest is *The Maid's Kid* of Tomotaka Tasaka, about a country girl who comes to work for a Tokyo family, an enormous step for a simple farm girl. In Imai's *Here is a Spring*, a group of young people, tired of doing nothing in a time when something should be done, organize an orchestra and go around giving concerts of Western music. It wasn't much, perhaps, what they did, but it was something.

124

Record of a Living Being, 1955, directed by Akira Kurosawa. TOP LEFT AND CENTER RIGHT: Toshiro Mifune and Takashi Shimura. BOTTOM LEFT: Kurosawa directing a scene.

THE FUTURE is by no means secure, particularly now, say the majority of Japanese, or the majority anywhere, for that matter. Kurosawa and his friends were considerably concerned about the 1955 H-Bomb experiments and produced *Record of a Living Being*, about a man obsessed by fear of atomic extinction.

TOP: *Human Torpedoes Attack*, 1955, directed by Takumi Furukawa, with Yujiro Ishihara (left) and Masayuki Mori (right). CENTER RIGHT: *The Private's Story*, 1955, directed by Seiichi Fukuda, with (from left) Achako Hanabishi, Junzaburo Ban, and Yumiko Miyagino. CENTER LEFT: *Weep, People of Japan—the Last Pursuit Plane*, 1956, directed by Hiroshi Noguchi.

THE WAR WAS by no means forgotten. In fact, another, the Korean War, had already begun, and one of Japan's official ambitions was that war would never again occur. The ways of regarding it, however, were many. One could show that it might be glorious but that it was terribly dangerous, as did *Human Torpedoes Attack*, or one could make fun of it, as in *The Private's Story;* one could pull its fangs by institutionalizing it, as did *God of War Admiral Yamamoto and the Combined Fleet*, or one could insist upon the loss and the horror, as in Hiroshi Noguchi's *Weep, People of Japan*. By far the strongest statement (and the best film), however, was found in Ichikawa's *The Harp of Burma*, a film which showed that one individual—a Japanese soldier who becomes a Buddhist monk—could indeed do something about war.

126

The Harp of Burma, 1956, directed by Kon Ichikawa,
with Shoji Yasui (foreground) and Rentaro Mikuni
(background center).

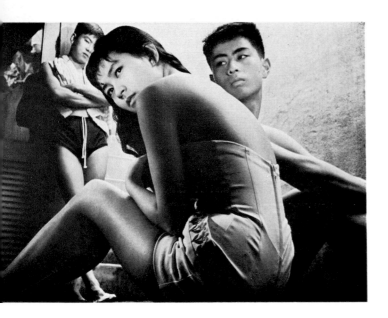

TOP LEFT: *Punishment Room*, 1956, directed by Kon Ichikawa, with Ayako Wakao (left) and Hiroshi Kawaguchi. RIGHT: *The Season of the Sun*, 1956, directed by Takumi Furukawa, with Yoko Minamida (left) and Hiroyuki Nagato. CENTER RIGHT: *Sun and Rose*, 1956, directed by Keisuke Kinoshita, with Katsuo Nakamura (right). LEFT: *Crazed Fruit*, 1956, directed by Ko Nakahira, with (from left) Yujiro Ishihara, Mie Kitahara, and Masahiko Tsugawa.

ANOTHER way of coping with the future is to examine the present with meticulous realism, particularly those aspects of it which seem to hold promise, and especially the promise of revolution and tragedy. As in most other countries, the middle years of the 1950's saw a revolt on the part of youth. This was particularly pronounced in Japan, and a young novelist, Shintaro Ishihara, became the spokesman for the discontented generation. He also saw most of his novels made into films. The best was probably Ichikawa's *Punishment Room*, about a young rebel who raped his girlfriend and told his father off (the latter, if not the former, extremely shocking in 1956 Japan). Others were *The Season of the Sun*, the extremely sensual *Crazed Fruit*, and Kinoshita's atypically violent *Sun and Rose*.

128

TOP LEFT: *Underwater Romance*, 1957, directed by Manao Horiguchi. TOP RIGHT: *The Woman by the Lonely Sea*, 1958, directed by Kosho Nomura. RIGHT: *Red Panties*, 1959, directed by Tsuruo Iwama.

ABOUT THE same time came the first of the nudies. There had long been, since the days of the Butterfly Dance, a number of such pictures, but this was the first time that big and respectable companies (such as Shochiku) made them. Unlike later pictures, which came to show naked ladies for their own very self-sufficient sake, these had story-lines. Naked girl diver is saved by hero from economic oppression / thugs / octopus. In only ten years Japan had come a long way from that first umbrella-shielded kiss.

129

TOP LEFT: *Three Kinds of Girls*, 1958, directed by Toshio Sugie, with (from left) Chiemi Eri, Izumi Yukimura, and Hibari Misora. TOP RIGHT: *Three Dolls in Ginza*, 1959, directed by Toshio Sugie, with (from left) Sonomi Nakajima, Reiko Dan, and Noriko Shigeyama. RIGHT: *Three Dolls Go to Hongkong*, 1959, directed by Toshio Sugie, with (from left) Sonomi Nakajima, Reiko Dan, and Noriko Shigeyama.

MUCH MORE popular, and more to the Japanese taste (a relatively refined one in that it finds a clothed lady also attractive) were the series of three-girl pictures which Toho began manufacturing. These were cannily designed to appeal to everyone. Hibari Misora was the traditional one, given to kimono, sentimental Japanese songs, flower arranging, etc.; Izumi Yukimura was the modern one who liked be-bop and got a big laugh by shouting that she had never worn a kimono in her life; and Chiemi Eri was the boyish, comic, all-willing country-girl. Their efforts (musical comedies with story-lines) proved so popular that a new series of three-girl films was later instituted with different actresses but the proportions about the same. One difference was in the titles, however. The earlier series had referred to three *musumé*, a word which connotes respectability, gentility. The latter called the girls *o-néchan*, a snappy Ginza-type word for girl which implies at least a certain amount of up-to-date looseness. In this series the boys didn't get them so much as *they* got the boys.

130

TOP LEFT: *Darkness at Noon*, 1956, directed by Tadashi Imai, with Sachiko Hidari (left) and Kojiro Kusanagi.
TOP RIGHT: Imai directing Hidari and Taketoshi Naito.
RIGHT: *I'll Buy You*, 1956, directed by Masaki Kobayashi, with Eijiro Tono (left) and Keiji Sada.

AMONG THE many moral changes which have occurred in Japan since the war, one of the most interesting has been the growth of social consciousness. Traditional Japan is notoriously lacking in it. This remains the country where one's garden is clipped with scissors, but the dead cat in the street in front is left until it dissolves; where the tea-ceremony master will perform in the house with the most rarified of manners but, on the way home, will publicly relieve himself in the street outside. In a country such as this, with its rigid dichotomy between private and public behavior, one would not expect that man should be his brother's keeper. In films, however, one often finds public injustice disclosed. One of the earlier was Kobayashi's *I'll Buy You*, about shameless goings-on in the midst of Japan's national sport—baseball. *Darkness at Noon* was about a then-current trial. The film reached the verdict of not guilty quite a few years before the courts finally did.

TOP LEFT: *Flowing*, 1956, directed by Mikio Naruse, with Isuzu Yamada (left) and Sumiko Kurishima. RIGHT: *Night River*, 1956, directed by Kozaburo Yoshimura, with Ken Uehara (left) and Fujiko Yamamoto. CENTER: *Red-Light District*, 1956, directed by Kenji Mizoguchi. LEFT: (from left) Machiko Kyo, Aiko Mimasu, Ayako Wakao, Kumeko Urabe, Sadako Sawamura and Eitaro Shindo. RIGHT: Mizoguchi with hsi cast

MIZOGUCHI's last film, *Red-Light District*—he died shortly after making it— was about the poor prostitutes of the country, and though the girls were not all that unhappy (as happenings after the anti-prostitution bill was passed indicated), the picture was one of the director's finest. Its final close-up of the tremulous face of a young girl on her first night is one which will long be remembered, as will the unsentimental and meticulously realistic delineation of the girls' lives. Like *Sansho* and *Oharu*, the film was actually about the Japanese woman and her struggles to find herself in a male-oriented world. Yoshimura's *Night River* had much the same theme: a well-born and modern-minded Kyoto girl runs directly into her own limitations. The most beautiful of all was Naruse's *Flowing*, about an older geisha, her daughter, and the family servant. The extraordinary wordless coda to this film, showing the women unaware of what we know will happen to them, then showing the river along which the geisha house is located, then showing the river flowing to the sea, is one of the most powerful evocations of *mono no awaré* on film.

132

THERE WERE other ways of showing woman's problems. Kobayashi in *Fountain* suggested that they were woman's fault; Naruse's *Kisses* suggested that they were the men's fault; and Shiro Toyoda, in a delightful comedy based on a Tanizaki novel, *A Cat, Shozo, and Two Women*, suggested that, no matter whose fault, they were quite funny. At the end of this picture, the hero, pursued by a parody of the traditional Japanese female on one hand and a travesty of modern girl on the other, much prefers his pet cat and in the end runs away with it.

CENTER LEFT: *Fountain*, 1956, directed by Masaki Kobayashi, with Keiji Sada (left) and Ineko Arima. RIGHT: *Kisses*, 1956, directed by Mikio Naruse, with Kyoko Aoyama and Hiroshi Tachikawa. BOTTOM: *A Cat, Shozo, and Two Women*, 1956, directed by Shiro Toyoda, with Kyoko Kagawa (left) and Hisaya Morishige.

133

TOP LEFT: *Extreme Sadness*, 1956, directed by Jukichi Uno, with Kinuyo Tanaka (second from left) and Kinzo Shin (right). RIGHT: Uno directing. LEFT: *Clouds at Twilight*, 1956, directed by Keisuke Kinoshita, with Shinji Tanaka (right) and Yuko Mochizuki.

THE PROBLEM of Japanese women is really the problem of everyone in Japan. When a person tries to realize himself (economically or spiritually) he keeps running into "society." This can be viewed as sad, a view taken by the appositely named *Extreme Sadness*, directed by actor Jukichi Uno, and by Kinoshita in his excellent study of young provincial life, *Clouds at Twilight*. Or it can be viewed as merely inevitable, the position taken by two minor Ozu pictures, *Early Spring* and *Tokyo Twilight*.

TOP LEFT: *Early Spring*, 1956, directed by Yasujiro Ozu, with Keiko Kishi (left) and Ryo Ikebe. RIGHT: Ozu directing a scene. BOTTOM LEFT: *Tokyo Twilight*, 1957, directed by Yasujiro Ozu, with Setsuko Hara (left) and Ineko Arima. RIGHT: Ozu directing a scene.

TOP LEFT: *A Story of Pure Love*, 1957, directed by Tadashi Imai, with Shinjiro Ehara (left) and Hitomi Nakahara. CENTER LEFT: *Downtown*, 1957, directed by Yasuke Chiba, with Toshiro Mifune (left) and Isuzu Yamada. RIGHT: *Times of Joy and Sorrow*, 1957, directed by Keisuke Kinoshita, with Keiji Sada (left) and Hideko Takamine.

THE PROBLEMS of being Japanese are also to be seen as tragic in Chiba's excellent *Downtown*, about a poor woman who finally finds someone who understands her only to lose him in a truck accident; or—a very radical approach—one may clamor against the injustice of it all, which is what Imai is always doing and which he did particularly energetically in *A Story of Pure Love*. In it he even changed the illness of the heroine from tuberculosis to atomic radiation. The most typical of Japanese reactions, however, is found in a film such as Kinoshita's long chronicle of a couple, man and wife, who tend lighthouses. The substance of the picture is sufficiently indicated by the title, *Times of Joy and Sorrow*. Such bitter-sweet combinations do seem authentically Japanese, at least to the extent that such films always win the yearly Ministry of Education film prizes.

136

COMMENT rather than criticism is usually the way with Japanese films. *Night Butterflies* was a look into the fascinating life of the Ginza bar-hostesses; *Black River* was a look at the world of pimps and whores which centers around U.S. military bases in the country. These films did not say that hostesses are good or that whores are bad, or the other way about: they simply observed the phenomena. Naruse's *Untamed*, a lovely Taisho-period film, observed something even rarer, the "modern girl" who is going to get what she wants, no matter what; and the final scene finds her, battered but unbowed, still trying.

CENTER LEFT: *Night Butterflies*, 1957, directed by Kozaburo Yoshimura, with (from left) Mieko Kondo, Eitaro Ozawa, (foreground) Machiko Kyo, and Fujiko Yamamoto. RIGHT: *Black River*, 1957, directed by Masaki Kobayashi, with Tatsuya Nakadai (left) and Ineko Arima. LEFT: *Untamed*, 1957, directed by Mikio Naruse, with (center table) Hideko Takamine and Masayuki Mori.

TOP LEFT: *Snow Country*, 1957, directed by Shiro Toyoda, with Ryo Ikebe (left) and Keiko Kishi. RIGHT: *An Osaka Story*, 1957, directed by Kozaburo Yoshimura, with Ganjuro Nakamura (left) and Kyoko Kagawa. CENTER: *A Tale of Dung and Urine*, 1957, directed by Yoshitaro Nomura, with Junzaburo Ban.

THIS IS more or less how the willful geisha acts in Toyoda's *Snow Country*, based on Yasunari Kawabata's most famous novel. Such striving for individuality is at odds with the family system, and this was what Yoshimura showed in *An Osaka Story*, a very lovingly detailed *shomin-geki* which was to have been directed by Mizoguchi. This film saw the dilemma as at least potentially tragic. Yoshitaro Nomura's aptly titled *A Tale of Dung and Urine* saw the plight of the individual as very funny indeed, particularly if he turns and, as in the glorious finale of this picture, does just what all individuals would really like to do to the indifferent world. The picture indicates this better than words can describe.

138

TOP: *Rice*, 1957, directed by Tadashi Imai, with Masako Nakamura (left) and Yuko Mochizuki. CENTER: *A Candle in the Wind*, 1957, directed by Keisuke Kinoshita, with (from left) Akiko Tamura, Hideko Takamine and Keiji Sada.

MORE OFTEN than not, it is the world that does it to the individual, which is what the poor mother discovers in *Rice* when she wades out to drown herself. The pathos here, however, was somewhat counteracted by all-location photography and the most meticulous delineation of peasant life since *Earth*. Kinoshita's *A Candle in the Wind* was also about a family in difficult straights. Returning to the manner of his earlier pictures, the director made one of his funniest satires on the family system.

The Throne of Blood, 1957, directed by Akira Kurosawa. TOP: Isuzu Yamada (left) and Toshiro Mifune. CENTER AND RIGHT: two other scenes.

140

The Lower Depths, 1957, directed by Akira Kuro-
sawa. TOP: Toshiro Mifune (left) and Kyoko Kagawa.
CENTER LEFT: Koji Mitsui. RIGHT: Mifune (left) and
Isuzu Yamada.

OF ALL JAPANESE directors, only Kurosawa and Ozu have taken the particular difficulties of being Japanese and enlarged them to include the truly
international difficulty of being at all. That their pictures and some of
Mizoguchi, Naruse, and others, should be about the problems of existence
in an age (and art) not usually given to such reflection indicates the seriousness of at least a minority of Japanese. Kurosawa's theme has been the
continued problem of evil in the world—or, to put it in a less negative way,
the possibilities of self-affirmation, given courage and patience and knowledge. What not to do was shown in that splendid adaptation from Shakespeare, *The Throne of Blood*, and in the almost equally excellent Gorky adaptation, *The Lower Depths*, two darkly beautiful pictures about the human
condition as it is but not necessarily as it must be.

141

The Hidden Fortress, 1958, directed by Akira Kurosawa.
TOP: Kamatari Fujiwara (left) and Minoru Chiaki.
BELOW: Toshiro Mifune.

HAVING DEFINED evil in his two adaptations from Shakespeare and Gorky, Kurosawa next created one of his most delightful pictures, an action fairy tale, as it were, about how funny evil is—a very fruitful path he followed through to *Yojimbo* and *Sanjuro*. This was *The Hidden Fortress*. Kinoshita also made a fairy tale in *The Ballad of the Narayama*, a picture which (using all sorts of devices from the kabuki) was based on a pseudo folktale about the sons of a village being forced to leave their aged mothers to die on mountaintops. The implied criticism of feudal ways was seen much more strongly in Tadashi Imai's excellent *Night-Drum*, an intricately-made picture about a man who makes his wife pay society's price for her adultery and then discovers that in so doing he has lost everything.

142

TOP AND CENTER: *The Ballad of the Narayama*, 1958, directed by Keisuke Kinoshita, with (from left) Teiji Takahashi and Kinuyo Tanaka. *Night-Drum*, 1958, directed by Tadashi Imai. BOTTOM LEFT: Rentaro Mikuni (left) and Ineko Arima. RIGHT: Imai directing the scene.

143

LEFT, TOP TO BOTTOM: *The Red Cloak*, 1958, directed by Teinosuke Kinugasa, with Ineko Arima (left) and Kanzaburo Nakamura; *Nichiren*, 1958, directed by Kunio Watanabe, with (from left) Yataro Kurokawa, Kazuo Hasegawa, Shoji Umewaka and Shintaro Katsu: *The Three Treasures*, 1958, directed by Hiroshi Inagaki, with Nobuko Otowa (foreground); *The Enchantress*, 1958, directed by Eisuke Takizawa, with Yumeji Tsukioka (left) and Ryoji Hayama. RIGHT, TOP TO BOTTOM: *The Life of Buddha*, 1962, directed by Kenji Misumi; *The Emperor Meiji and the Russo-Japanese Great War*, 1957, directed by Kunio Watanabe; *The Great Wall of China*, 1962, directed by Shigeo Tanaka.

144

Four versions of *The Loyal Forty-seven Ronin* (*Chushingura*). TOP LEFT: 1938, directed by Masahiro Makino and Tomiyasu Ikeda, with Chiezo Kataoka. RIGHT: 1954, directed by Tatsuo Osone, with Kokichi Takada (center). CENTER LEFT: 1957, directed by Tatsuo Osone, with Yataro Kitagami (left). RIGHT: 1962, directed by Hiroshi Inagaki, with Yuzo Kayama (second from left).

THE LINES between the period film, the fairy-tale film, and the epic are always nebulous, but the Japanese industry rather smudged them in a series of all-star-cast block busters. The best was the comedy-epic, *The Red Cloak*, starring Kanzaburo Nakamura, the famous kabuki actor. The perennial epic is *The Loyal Forty-seven Ronin*, of which, from the first Matsunosuke version, there have been dozens.

145

TOP: *The Human Condition*, 1958, directed by Masaki Kobayashi, with Tatsuya Nakadai. RIGHT: *The Rickshaw Man*, 1958, directed by Hiroshi Inagaki, with Toshiro Mifune.

A MODERN epic was Masaki Kobayashi's *The Human Condition*, a three-part film based on a best-selling novel about Japan's brutal exploitation of Manchuria before the second world war. It was so direct and so honest that the Japanese government was (initially, at any rate) rather unhappy at its going abroad. In Germany, playing under the title *Barfuss durch die Hölle*, it set postwar attendance records. Another Japanese film popular abroad was the lesser *The Rickshaw Man*, a pale (if highly-colored) remake which reminded—comfortingly it would appear—of *Stella Dallas*.

TOP LEFT: *Lucky Dragon, No. 5*, 1958, directed by Kaneto Shindo, with Jukichi Uno (right). RIGHT: *The Naked Sun*, 1958, directed by Miyoji Ieki. with Shinjiro Ehara (left). CENTER LEFT: *Kiku and Isamu*, 1958, directed by Tadashi Imai. RIGHT: *The Naked Face of Night*, 1958, directed by Kozaburo Yoshimura, with Ayako Wakao (left) and Machiko Kyo.

As CRITICAL as *The Human Condition*, and more topical, were Imai's *Kiku and Isamu*, about mixed-blood children, one of the less publicized legacies of the Occupation, and Kaneto Shindo's *Lucky Dragon, No. 5,* about the tuna-fisherman who strayed into the Bikini A-bomb testing zone. Americans were largely blamed for both. In *The Naked Sun*, however, Japanese big business came in for a drubbing. Yoshimura's *The Naked Face of Night* took on the elegant intrigues in the world of classical Japanese dance; and *The Naked General*, though a comedy based on the life and work of a well-known and very talented though mentally retarded artist, managed a few deserved slaps at "sane" complacency.

THE WARPED mind, not often seen in Japanese films (and hardly treated sympathetically since *A Page Out of Order*) was the pretext for *Conflagration*, Ichikawa's treatment of the Mishima novel, *The Temple of the Golden Pavilion*, and one of the most exciting of all postwar films. In this dark and evocative picture about the boy who burned down the priceless pavilion, the director managed to suggest (without saying so) that it is the world which is warped, certainly more than those who destroy for love.

Conflagration, 1958, directed by Kon Ichikawa. CENTER LEFT: Raizo Ichikawa (left) and Tatsuya Nakadai. RIGHT: Raizo Ichikawa (left). BOTTOM: Raizo Ichikawa (left) and Ganjiro Nakamura.

148

TOP LEFT: *Baby Carriage*, 1958, directed by Tomotaka Tasaka, with (from left) Izumi Ashikawa, Hisako Yamane, Jukichi Uno, Yujiro Ishihara, and Michiyo Aratama. RIGHT: *Street in the Sun*, 1958, directed by Tomotaka Tasaka, with Koreya Senda (left) and Yujiro Ishihara. CENTER LEFT: *Anzukko*, 1958, directed by Mikio Naruse, with Ko Kimura (left) and Kyoko Kagawa. RIGHT: *Children of the Composition Class*, 1958, directed by Seiji Hisamatsu, with Kyoko Kagawa (right).

ONE OF THE strengths of the Japanese film—and of the Japanese people— is that things are celebrated with something of the same strength that these same things are (less occasionally) criticized. In the West, critical films are usually strong, and "celebration" films (*Andy Hardy*, etc.) are weak. Western films about unlucky lovers tend to be honest; films about happy lovers tend to be vapid and sentimental. In Japan, however, the emotion to affirm things like young love and happy families is a very real and hence a very strong one. Saved from cynicism and often from sentimentality as well, a director like Tomotaka Tasaka, in films such as *Baby Carriage* and *Street in the Sun*, can carry his "up-lift" message with perfect poise because he believes in it. Such Naruse pictures as *Anzukko* and *Herringbone Clouds* are dignified by the same belief. Even those which point out flaws (unresponsive adults in *Children of the Composition Class*, an impossible mother in the very amusing *Four Seasons of Love*) do so with the belief that people after all do lead interesting lives, even beautiful ones.

149

TOP: *The Four Seasons of Love*, 1958, directed by Ko Nakahira, with Isuzu Yamada (left), and Sanae Naka-hara. RIGHT: *Herringbone Clouds*, 1958, directed by Mikio Naruse. with Ganjiro Nakamura (left) and Keiju Kobayashi.

IN THE LATER FILMS of Ozu this "celebration" of the way things are is elevated to a rite, almost indeed an apotheosis. Even in lesser pictures such as *Equinox Flower* (Ozu's first color film) and *Good Morning* (a color and sound remake of *I Was Born, But...*) the extraordinary tact of this director, his love and affection for his characters, create utterly memorable experiences. In his finest pictures, *Late Spring*, *Tokyo Story*, and *Flowing Weeds*, the beauty of these resigned people becomes more than moving; it becomes stirring, because we see in this beautiful resignation a philosophy, a metaphysics, which suddenly seems quite right—and so very close to what a human being can experience, what a human being is about. Ozu's films (with their long cuts, their extra-ordinary leisure) are not slow; and, though filled with the stuff most directors attempt to make tragedy of, are not unhappy. They are, rather, profoundly beautiful, profoundly honest.

150

151

THE SUPERLATIVELY polished surface of the Ozu film reveals its depths. Many of the best Japanese films, however, are no deeper than their surfaces, and this does not imply shallowness so much as that the motion picture which presents the skin of life is also—even equally—valid. Many of Kinugasa's later films are examples of this; *The White Heron*, for example. So is Toyoda's lovely *Pilgrimage at Night*. One of the most delightful of these pictures is Inagaki's making of Rostand's *Cyrano de Bergerac*—a completely superficial play—into an amusing and elegant film, *The Life Story of a Certain Swordsman*.

CENTER: *The White Heron*, 1959, directed by Teinosuke Kinugasa, with Fujiko Yamamoto. BOTTOM LEFT: *Pilgrimage at Night*, 1959, directed by Shiro Toyoda, with Fujiko Yamamoto and Ryo Ikebe (from left on footbridge). BELOW: *The Life of a Certain Swordsman*, 1959, directed by Hiroshi Inagaki, with Yoko Tsukasa (left) and Toshiro Mifune.

TOP: *Nianchan*, 1959, directed by Shohei Imamura, with Hiroyuki Nagato (second from left). CENTER RIGHT: *I Want to Be a Shellfish*, 1959, directed by Shinobu Hashimoto, with Michiyo Aratama (left) and Frankie Sakai. LEFT: *A Town of Love and Hate*, 1959, directed by Nagisa Oshima.

PICTURES which only superficially criticize fall into a less pleasant category. Having set out to expose, the exposure is expected to be complete, and something like disappointment is felt if it is any less than that. *Nianchan* was going to be about the horrors of being a coal miner in Kyushu; *I Want To Be a Shellfish* (directed by Shinobu Hashimoto, one of Japan's best scenarists and scripter of *Rashomon*) was going to be about unfair Allied Occupation war criminal trials; *A Town of Love and Hate* (the debut film of Nagisa Oshima) was going to be about the general corruption and decadence of Tokyo life. Something happened to them, as indeed happens perhaps oftener in Japan than elsewhere to films which aim to be critical.

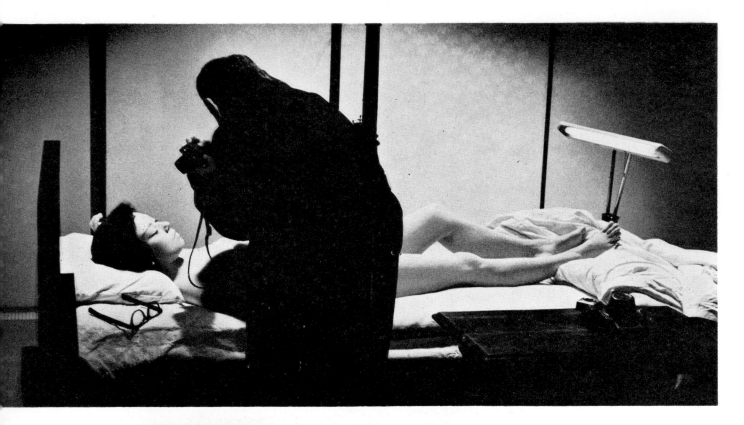

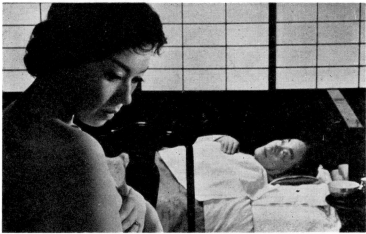

The Key, 1959, directed by Kon Ichikawa. Scenes with Machiko Kyo and
Ganjiro Nakamura.

Two of Kon Ichikawa's films criticized profoundly, and part of the success
of these pictures is that he did not bother with only Tokyo corruption; he
implied corruption everywhere in *The Key*, a film which was on one level a
macabre comedy about Japanese family life and, on another level, about
the various kinds of obsessions we cultivate (hence the English running-title,
Odd Obsession) to keep from facing ourselves in all of our naked loneliness.
Somewhat the same theme dignified that most powerful of all Japanese
anti-war films, *Fires on the Plain*. Its difference from two other anti-war films
of the period, *The Last of the Imperial Army* and Kinoshita's *The River Fuefuki*,
was that it was not content merely to *say* that war was bad: it showed it. Few
who have seen the Ichikawa film will forget the horror of the march in the
rain or the pathos of the final scene; the last soldier, hands in the air, going
to give himself up, believing he will be killed and no longer caring.

154

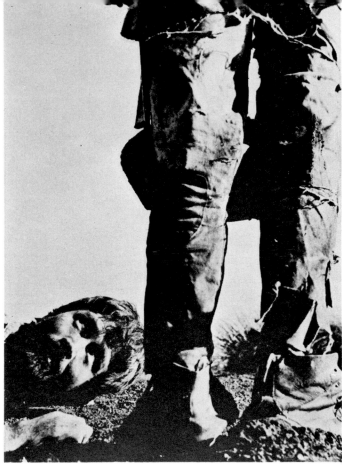

TOP: *Fires on the Plain*, 1959, directed by Kon Ichikawa, with Eiji Funakoshi. CENTER: *Last of the Imperial Army*, 1960, directed by Masuichi Iizuka, with Rentaro Mikuni (left) and Ko Kimura. BOTTOM LEFT: *The River Fuefuki*, 1960, directed by Keisuke Kinoshita, with Hideko Takamine (left).

155

TOP AND CENTER LEFT: *The Bad Sleep Well*, 1960, directed by Akira Kurosawa, with Toshiro Mifune. RIGHT: *Black Book*, 1960, directed by Hiromichi Horikawa, with Keiju Kobayashi.

IN JAPAN, as in other countries, it is easier to be critical of things like the lot of the poor and the corruption of big cities than to be specific about the causes. Kurosawa in *The Bad Sleep Well* attacked the Establishment itself and suggested (what everyone knows but what rarely appears on film) that the corruption of the big business combines was directly linked to equal corruption in the government. In *Black Book*, Horikawa, Kurosawa's some-time-assistant-director, criticized Japanese courts, and Oshima's *Cruel Stories of Youth* attacked the only partially dismantled feudal structure of Tokyo gang-life and made the telling comment that Japanese big business and Japanese criminal establishments share the same assumptions.

156

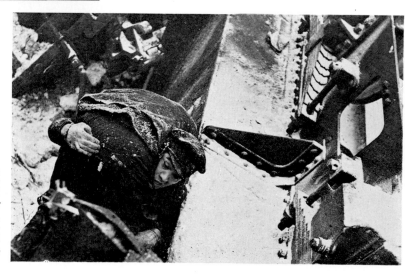

TOP: *Cruel Stories of Youth*, 1960, directed by Nagisa Oshima, with Yusuke Kawazu (left) and Miyuki Kuwano. CENTER: *The Grave of the Sun*, 1960, directed by Nagisa Oshima, with Yusuke Kawazu (right). BOTTOM: *The Great Road*, 1960, directed by Hideo Sekigawa, with Rentaro Mikuni.

157

Bonchi, 1960, directed by Kon Ichikawa. TOP: Raizo Ichikawa (background). CENTER LEFT: (from left) Kikue Mori, Isuzu Yamada and Ichikawa.

ONE OF THE feudal remains was the presumed low position of women. By fifteen years after the end of the war, however, it had become apparent that the lot of Japanese women had improved to the point that (as in America) she was gaining economic control, at least in the home. Ichikawa's excellent *Bonchi* was about matriarchy: mother and daughter combine to rule the love life of the latter's son, the last of his line. In the same director's *Younger Brother*, it is the mother who rules and the children who suffer, a welcome and novel switch from the usual Japanese family-life film. Ko Nakahira's hour-long *Assignation* shows the neglected wife most unsympathetically. First she picks up a younger student and then, when he wants to leave her, kills him. Yoshimura's *A Fence of Women* showed how the "new" Japanese women acted among each other, scarcely a reassuring sight for the Japanese male who, in all of these pictures, had shattered some of his most cherished illusions about that mythical creature, the much put-upon, acquiescent Japanese woman.

158

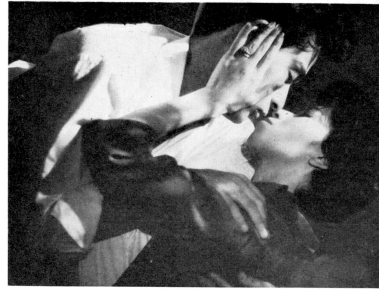

TOP: *Younger Brother*, 1960, directed by Kon Ichikawa, with Keiko Kishi (left) and Hiroshi Kawaguchi. CENTER: *Assignation*, 1960, directed by Yasushi Nakahira, with Takao Ito (left) and Yoko Katsuragi. BOTTOM: *A Fence of Women*, 1960, directed by Kozaburo Yoshimura, with Momoko Kochi (left) and Mariko Okada.

159

TOP: *When a Woman Ascends the Stairs*, 1960, directed by Mikio Naruse, with Hideko Takamine (center). CENTER LEFT: *Flowing Night*, 1960, directed by Mikio Naruse, with Isuzu Yamada. CENTER RIGHT: *Autumn Is Beginning*, 1960, directed by Mikio Naruse. BOTTOM: *Mother, Wife, Daughter*, 1960, directed by Mikio Naruse, with Hideko Takamine (second from right).

THE HEROINE of Naruse's *When a Woman Ascends the Stairs*, somewhat like the girl in the same director's *Untamed*, knows what she wants and sets out to get it. She owns an upstairs Ginza bar (hence the title) and knows perfectly well how to counterfeit the smiling acquiescence which her profession demands. Three other Naruse pictures, *Autumn Is Beginning*, *Flowing Night*, and *Mother, Wife, Daughter*, were, in varying degrees, about the way women really are. Their tragedy, as seen in these films, is that they allow their idea of duty (proper marriage, being a "good wife") to win over their inclination (becoming themselves, realizing themselves as people). This is a real dilemma (not only in the kabuki, and not only in Japan) and Naruse is one of the direc-

TOP: *Late Autumn*, 1960, directed by Yasujiro Ozu, with Setsuko Hara (left) and Yoko Tsukasa. CENTER: *Naked Island*, 1960, directed by Kaneto Shindo, with Nobuko Otowa.

tors who most brilliantly treats it. Two contrasting pictures of women are seen in Ozu's *Late Autumn* and in Kaneto Shindo's *Naked Island*. In the former picture (a color remake of *Late Spring*) mother and daughter live together, and the former decides that the girl must live her own life. In the latter picture the peasant woman is doing just that, and it is difficult, backbreaking labor that her life is made of. Despite the fact that Ozu was celebrating family life and Shindo was criticizing it, the picture of the Japanese woman which emerges from each of these strong films is equally cogent. One feels in each—well-brought-up girl and peasant woman—a kind of strength, of resiliency which, it must be said, Japanese men don't often have.

161

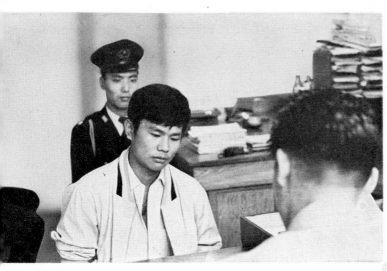

TOP AND CENTER RIGHT: *Bad Boys*, 1961, directed by
Susumu Hani. CENTER LEFT: *Pigs and Battleships*, di-
rected by Shohei Imamura, with (from left) Hiroyuki
Nagato, Takeshi Kato, and Tetsuro Tamba.

WHAT HAPPENS to boys when they try to lead their own lives was brilliantly
shown in the first feature of the young Susumu Hani, *Bad Boys*. A documentary using hidden cameras and non-actors, the picture shows a boy whose
efforts to escape from society land him in a reformatory. One of the many fine
things about this film was that there was no indication of regeneration; one
rather hoped he would indeed not go straight because to dare be yourself
in conformist Japan appears something like heroism—that is, if you have
some kind of character to begin with. Shohei Imamura's entertaining piece
of Grand Guignol, *Pigs and Battleships*, denied that his characters (several of
whom are eaten by pigs) had any at all.

162

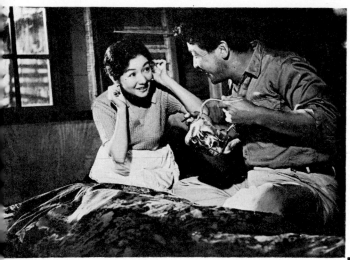

TOP: *The Happiness of Us Alone*, 1961, directed by Zenzo Matsuyama, with Hideko Takamine (left) and Keiju Kobayashi. CENTER RIGHT: *As a Wife, As a Woman*, 1961, directed by Mikio Naruse, with Choko Iida (left) and Hideko Takamine. BOTTOM: *The Bitter Spirit*, 1961, directed by Keisuke Kinoshita.

ONE OF THE most fruitful of all cinematic themes is provided when men bent on realizing themselves as people get together with women bent on the same thing. Zenzo Matsuyama, a disciple of Keisuke Kinoshita, showed in *The Happiness of Us Alone* that generosity and need could make a happy marriage, even if husband and wife were deaf and dumb. Naruse again showed the difficulty in the aptly titled *As a Wife, As a Woman*, and Kinoshita showed that men and women simply cannot get along and are not intended to in *The Bitter Spirit*.

163

TOP: *The Autumn of the Kohayagawa Family*, 1961, directed by Yasujiro Ozu, with Setsuko Hara (left) and Yoko Tsukasa. CENTER: *Apostasy*, 1961, directed by Kon Ichikawa, with Raizo Ichikawa (left) and Shiho Fujimura. BOTTOM: *Ten Dark Women*, 1961, directed by Kon Ichikawa, with Keiko Kishi (left) and Fujiko Yamamoto.

Ozu's *The Autumn of the Kohayagawa Family* was—more than is usual in an Ozu film—about the stresses and strains and rewards of marriage. Ichikawa's *Apostasy,* from the same source as the earlier Kinoshita film, was about the little-known fact of a caste system in Japan, and in it he strongly suggested that the lot of the pariah boy would have been extraordinarily eased if he and the girl could have gotten together, that together they might have been able to work out their problems. Or else—as in an extraordinarily black comedy, *Ten Dark Women*—it would have been the hilarious hell of a man whose wife, mistresses, and girlfriends conspire to murder him.

164

THE WORLD and its troubles are so much with us that Kurosawa took the extraordinary step of laughing at them in *Yojimbo*. This extremely funny period comedy laughed at personal ambition, personal involvement, and the whole feudal mess. Since the alternative to laughter is tears, and since Japanese film has been rich to satiation in the latter, this refreshing Kurosawa picture became one of his most popular. The hero is no better than his adversaries, but he, at least, knows how to make evil gobble up evil.

Yojimbo, 1961, directed by Akira Kurosawa. CENTER: Toshiro Mifune. BOTTOM LEFT: (from left) Mifune, Daisuke Kato, Tatsuya Nakadai and Eijiro Tono. RIGHT: Isuzu Yamada (right background) and Mifune (right).

165

THE KUROSAWA picture was, among other things, about the stupidity of war. Japan was now twenty years away from Pearl Harbor and its consequences. A number of films were made which looked back with some nostalgia to these times of horror. Since the audience was of an average age which could remember nothing of the event, they were appreciated as action films. The producers, remembering, managed to introduce a note of nostalgia or else a veiled hint of "never again." Both *The Zero Fighter* and *Five Charging Soldiers* had difficulty in reconciling the never-again with the daring-do that the films so obviously glorified. A much more sober appraisal of the mentality that allows war was seen in Masaki Kobayashi's excellent *Harakiri*, with a script by Shinobu Hashimoto that was one of the strongest of all anti-feudal statements.

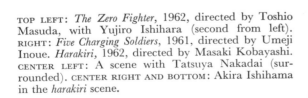

TOP LEFT: *The Zero Fighter*, 1962, directed by Toshio Masuda, with Yujiro Ishihara (second from left). RIGHT: *Five Charging Soldiers*, 1961, directed by Umeji Inoue. *Harakiri*, 1962, directed by Masaki Kobayashi. CENTER LEFT: A scene with Tatsuya Nakadai (surrounded). CENTER RIGHT AND BOTTOM: Akira Ishihama in the *harakiri* scene.

166

Sanjuro, 1962, directed by Akira Kurosawa. TOP: (from left), Toshiro Mifune Yuzo Kayama (on wall), and (foreground sitting) Takako Irie and Reiko Dan CENTER LEFT: Kurosawa directing. RIGHT: Mifune in the scene.

THE KOBAYASHI film was strong and dead serious. Its humanistic view of the cold intricacies of Tokugawa feudalism (and, by implication, their present-day remains) was passionately concerned. Just as strong was *Sanjuro*—but Akira Kurosawa chose to view Tokugawa Japan as high comedy. His boy samurai (who would ordinarily have grown into men as dangerous as those in the Kobayashi picture) meet a real, human samurai who, without really intending to, teaches them that life is a far different thing from the logistics of honor and obligation. Both pictures, though opposite in many ways, indicate an answer to a question which has long concerned Japan. The country's heritage includes six hundred years as a police state, one of the most efficient in the history of the world. It is now just a century over, and yet the mentality that it created still continues. The question is, what to do about it.

167

SHOWING THAT a feudal attitude is not entirely bad accounts for much of the popularity of *The Rickshaw Man*. Part—if not all—of its beauty is that the hero believes in the system of feudal rank, and how can he, a humble rickshaw-man, presume to love the well-born lady? Naruse's heroine in *A Record of Wandering* is a famous novelist, but she too believes in the ideas which complicate her love life. The same director's *A Woman Place*, as the title indicates, is about the place that a feudal society has made for her. Kinoshita's *The Ballad of a Workman* is about the working class and their attitude toward getting ahead in the world. Convinced of their own limitations, they don't.

TOP LEFT: *The Rickshaw Man*, 1962, directed by Shinji Murayama, with Rentaro Mikuni. RIGHT, TOP TO BOTTOM: *A Record of Wandering*, 1962, directed by Mikio Naruse, with Hideko Takamine (center). *A Woman's Place*, 1962, directed by Mikio Naruse, with Hideko Takamine (left) and Haruko Sugimura. *The Ballad of a Workman*, 1962, directed by Keisuke Kinoshita, with Keiji Sada (left) and Yoshiko Kuga.

168

TOP LEFT: *Mother Country*, 1962, directed by Keisuke Kinoshita, with (from left) Yoshiko Kuga, unidentified actor, Keiju Kobayashi, Miyuki Kuwano, Akira Ishihama, Hideko Takamine, and Mickey Curtis. CENTER LEFT: *The Inheritance*, 1962, directed by Masaki Kobayashi, with So Yamamura (left) and Keiko Kishi. RIGHT: *An Autumn Afternoon*, 1962, directed by Yasujiro Ozu, with (from left face showing) Nobuo Nakamura, Ryuji Kita, and Chishu Ryu.

THE DIFFERENCE between the generations in this matter is seen in another Kinoshita picture, *Mother Country*, about Hawaiian nisei and the old folks from Japan. Kobayashi's *The Inheritance* is, in a way, about the same thing. An older man is dying, and the younger people in his life gather about him, anxious not only for the money but also for some indication of what his feudal life in big business has been like. In most of these films, particularly the Kinoshita ones, a careful differentiation is made between the bad and the beautiful aspects of the feudal. Ozu, as always, finds all such questions beside the point, particularly in his last film, the beautiful *An Autumn Afternoon*. The Japanese are as they are, says Ozu, and this is how they act. This is something which exists; it need not be criticized nor explained, it is a fact. This placid, funny, lovely, elegiac final picture affirms an acceptance of the world as it is.

169

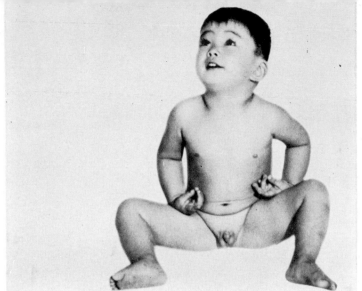

TOP: *I Am Two Years Old*, 1962, directed by Kon Ichikawa. CENTER LEFT: *The Foundry Town*, 1962, directed by Shoji Imamura, with Sayuri Yoshinaga (right). RIGHT: *Children Hand in Hand*, 1963, directed by Susumu Hani.

ACCEPTING the world as it is and accepting oneself in this world is a difficult thing to do and, in addition, is but one of the ways of living, the other being to try to change oneself and/or the world. The Japanese cinema, as well as the other Japanese arts, presents an oscillation between these poles. It is so manifest that one could even say that Ozu, Mizoguchi, and Naruse are on the ethical right, while Kurosawa, Kobayashi, and Ichikawa are on the ethical left. The latter began at the beginning in *I Am Two Years Old* and in this loving chronicling of the first two years of infancy suggested (through the members of the family—old-fashioned grandmother, modern-minded mother) that Baby had two roads, either of which he might travel. *The Foundry Town* showed an older girl, in her teens, deciding to live her own life in the city, and Susumu Hani's *Children Hand in Hand* indicated that the little hero was well on his way to becoming an individual.

170

ANOTHER Hani film, *A Full Life,* showed a girl having trouble finding out who she is. An actress involved in a liaison with a thoroughly attractive no-good, she finally breaks off with him and, at the end of the picture, is about to take up with a better older man. The picture is purposely ambivalent, however, and the title might be interpreted ironically. The girl, searching for herself, merely moves from one man to another.

A Full Life, 1962, directed by Susumu Hani. TOP: Ineko Arima. BOTTOM LEFT: Arima and I. George. RIGHT: Scene with Arima.

171

TOP LEFT: *A Human Being*, 1962, directed by Kaneto Shindo, with Nobuko Otowa (left) and Kei Sato. RIGHT, TOP TO BOTTOM: *That Woman from Osaka*, 1962, directed by Eizo Sugawa, with Reiko Dan and Kamatari Fujiwara (background, center and right). *A Lie*, 1962, directed by Teinosuke Kinugasa, with Nobuko Otowa (right). *Corrosion*, 1962, directed by Yasuzo Masumura, with Ayako Wakao (left) and Jiro Tamiya.

THE HEROINE of *That Woman from Osaka* moves among a great number of men. A re-make of Mizoguchi's *Osaka Elegy*, the picture sees that a girl has little choice, that the girl who can stand up alone is most uncommon and even, in Japan as elsewhere, unwanted. What women do to achieve their ends (falsehood, infidelity, etc.) was seen as funny in Kinugasa's light comedy, *Lies*, and as tragic in Masumura's very smart melodrama, *Corrosion*. Ladies in the admittedly unlikely circumstance of shipwreck were seen in Shindo's *A Human Being*. More shocking than that the hungry cast almost consume a small boy was that a woman proves stronger than the men and all but takes over the boat.

172

TOP: *The Body*, 1962, directed by Masahige Narusawa, with Michiko Saga (left) and Hiroyuki Nagato. *We Will Never Forget That Night*, 1962, directed by Kozaburo Yoshimura. CENTER LEFT: Yoshimura directing Ayako Wakao. RIGHT: Jiro Tamiya (left) and Wakao.

SOMETHING a bit more subtle than cannibalism was seen in the debut film of Masahige Narusawa called *The Body*, in which the young girl wakes up to the fact that she is sexually irresistible and begins a grand, comic, and completely unrepentant career. A girl with many more scruples was the Hiroshima survivor in *We Will Never Forget That Night*, who remains faithful to one man. Both, oddly, end somewhat the same way. The Hiroshima girl ends up a bar hostess, and in the deliciously ambivalent final scene of *The Body* the young heroine is toying with the idea of going the whole way and becoming a prostitute.

173

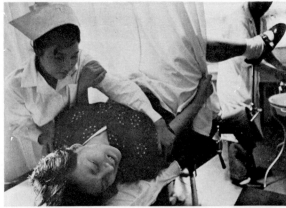

TOP LEFT: *Yearning*, 1963, directed by Mikio Naruse, with Hideko Takamine (left) and Yuzo Kayama. RIGHT, TOP TO BOTTOM: *Insect Woman*, 1963, directed by Shohei Imamura, with Sachiko Hidari (lying). *The Old Capital*, 1963, directed by Noboru Nakamura, with Shima Iwashita. *The Bamboo Doll*, 1963, directed by Kozaburo Yoshimura, with Junichiro Yamashita (center) and Ayako Wakao (right).

SUCH GIRLS are rare, which is one of the reasons *The Body* was so refreshing a film. Much more common, on the screen as in life, are those girls who are torn between what they want to do and what they think they should. In Naruse's *Yearning*, the heroine falls in love with the younger brother of her dead husband and fights against this emotion. In *Insect Woman*, the girl goes through almost everything (including prostitution and abortion) but at the end keeps on believing that she is different from what she has shown us she is. *The Old Capital*, a film very like Mizoguchi's *Sisters of the Gion*, finds the girl trying to be respectable and free at the same time, a combination which never works. In *The Bamboo Doll*, the girl is more and more forced to free herself because she cannot realize herself through an impotent if loving husband.

174

She and He, 1963, directed by Susumu Hani. TOP: Sachiko Hidari. CENTER LEFT: Hidari and Eiji Okada. RIGHT: Hidari and Hani.

ONE OF THE best statements of the problem was in Susumu Hani's *She and He*. The wife is not dissatisfied so much as that she feels, cooped up in her apartment house, that life is occurring outside the windows, away from her. She becomes friendly with a rag-picker and tries to help him and his adopted daughter. A number of incidents—each as inconclusive as life itself—occur, and she realizes that she is of no real help to anyone. Still, she wonders. The memorable final scene shows her in bed, her husband sound asleep. We do not know what she is thinking, but by now we can guess: she is wondering about life, wondering about herself.

175

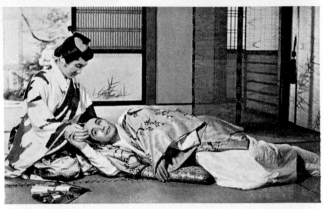

The Revenge of Yuki-no-jo, 1963, directed by Kon Ichikawa. TOP LEFT: Ayako Wakao (left) and Kazuo Hasegawa. TOP RIGHT: Ichikawa directing. *Cruel Tales of Bushido*, 1963, directed by Tadashi Imai. CENTER: Kinnosuke Nakamura (left) and Masayuki Mori. BOTTOM: Nakamura.

WOMEN OF course, do not have a monopoly on this problem. Everyone wonders who he is. But women are supposed to be acted upon and this is supposed to define them; men are supposed to act and this is supposed to define *them*. The problem is that we see-saw back and forth between what we want to be and what we are (a motion that has been called, among other things, the wheel of *karma*). A somewhat bizarre solution was arranged by Kon Ichikawa in *The Revenge of Yuki-no-jo*, the hero of which is a female impersonator, somewhat like those found in the early days of Japanese cinema. Both acting and acted upon, he seemed to double his chances of eventual self-identification. Tadashi Imai suggested another solution: you break the fatal circle, you stop the wheel. In his *Cruel Tales of Bushido*, he follows his hero through seven incarnations. In each, the man suffers because what he is (e.g., a loyal vassal) is incompatible with what he wants to be (a free man). In the last—now—he braves the big boss and marries the girl.

176

White and Black, 1963, directed by Hiromichi Horikawa. TOP LEFT: Keiju Kobayashi (left) and Horikawa (directing). RIGHT: Tatsuya Nakadai. CENTER LEFT: *Tokyo Bay*, 1963, directed by Yoshitaro Nomura. RIGHT: *Legacy of the Five Hundred Thousand*, 1963, directed by and starring Toshiro Mifune.

A LESS DIRECT way of defining personal potential is to realize the extent of one's responsibility. The idea of personal responsibility is a new one in Japan. The heros in *The Loyal Forty-seven Rōnin* take responsibility and even slit themselves open, but they are not truly personally involved; they are behaving as they "must." A man's realizing that he is truly responsible for the actions of others is a very different thing. In *White and Black*, Horikawa made a film about the necessity of confession, even when one is not guilty of the crime he is accused of. *Tokyo Bay* was a parable about the "guilty" one and the "innocent" one and purposely confused the two. *The Legacy of the Five Hundred Thousand*, directed by Toshiro Mifune, was about a group of ex-soldiers who examine their consciences as they search for the cache left behind in the Philippines.

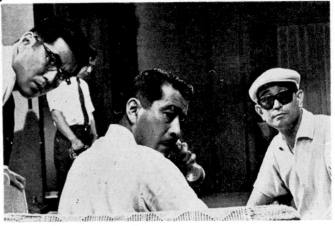

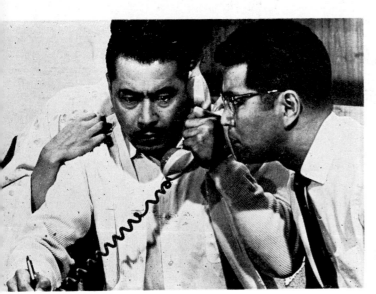

High and Low, 1963, directed by Akira Kurosawa. TOP:
Toshiro Mifune (left) and Tsutomu Yamazaki. CENTER
RIGHT: (from left) Tatsuya Mihashi, Mifune, and
Kurosawa. LEFT: Mifune and Mihashi.

THESE NEW pictures about personal responsibility all took the form of the
action melodrama, the cops-and-robbers thriller which, in all countries, so
fits the search for identity and responsibility. The final word, however, was
Kurosawa's metaphysical thriller, *High and Low*. A perfectly nice, quite
ordinary man is ruined when his chauffeur's son is kidnapped and he must
pay the ransom. At the end of the film he confronts the kidnapper. Kurosawa
shoots this final scene in such a way that the reflection of the prison glass
fuses the two faces. Good is responsible for evil; the example of the good man
caused envy and hate. He *is* responsible.

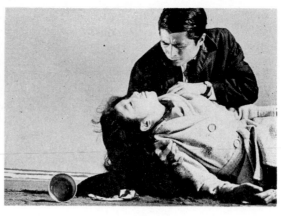

TOP LEFT: *A Public Benefactor*, 1964, directed by Satsuo Yamamoto, with So Yamamura (left) and Eiko Taki. RIGHT: *The Mark of Evil*, 1964, directed by Hiromichi Horikawa, with Kyoko Kishida (lying) and Tsutomu Yamazaki. CENTER RIGHT: *Pale Flower*, 1964, directed by Masahiro Shinoda. LEFT: *The Black Sun*, 1964, directed by Koreyoshi Kurahara, with Chiko Lourant (left) and Tamio Kawaji.

THIS IS very hard-boiled reasoning indeed, particularly for the Japanese, a people notoriously prone to shift the blame and pass the buck. Other investigations into the fascinating tangle of evil were Satsuo Yamamoto's blistering attack on big business in *A Public Benefactor*, and Horikawa's study of revenge, *The Mark of Evil*. In *Pale Flower*, Masahiro Shinoda made his debut with a strange and dream-like picture of gambling dens and a perfectly amoral girl, a kind of bad *princesse lointain*.

179

A MORE ORDINARY view of evil is that it is inherent rather than caused, that conditions foster it. This was the view of *The Black Sun*, about the odd relationship between a young Japanese jazz fan and an A.W.O.L. American Negro soldier. Imamura's *Intentions of Murder* was about a young wife raped by a burglar. Knowing this to be wrong, she still likes it. She is responsible, then, for the continued liaison, but (as in all Imamura's films) the implication is that somehow society caused it all. Imai's study of rape and murder, *A Story of Echigo*, did not involve society but said that the villain was simply a bad man. This is the ordinary way of looking at the problem of evil, and the differences between this view and that of Kurosawa are apparent.

Intentions of Murder, 1964, directed by Shohei Imamura. CENTER LEFT: Masumi Harukawa. RIGHT: Imamura directing. BOTTOM LEFT: *The Scent of Incense*, 1964, directed by Keisuke Kinoshita, with (standing from left) Mariko Okada and Eiji Okada. RIGHT: *A Story of Echigo*, 1964, directed by Tadashi Imai, with Yoshiko Sakuma (lying) and Shoichi Ozawa.

180

TOP LEFT: *The Sound of Waves*, 1964, directed by Kenjiro Morinaga, with Sayuri Yoshinaga (left) and Mitsuo Hamada. RIGHT: *Manji*, 1964, directed by Yasuzo Masumura, with Ayako Wakao (left) and Kyoko Kishida. *Onibaba*, 1964, directed by Kaneto Shindo. CENTER LEFT: Shindo directing. RIGHT: Nobuko Otowa (left) and Jitsuko Yoshimura.

BUT THEN it is a rare director in any country who shows that the self is to blame and not the outside world. The Japanese, like most people, continue to cling to the belief that the world is arranged so that various injustices can occur, and for this reason, the cold and unfriendly world has long played a major part in Japanese cinema. An example was Kinoshita's three-hour-long *The Scent of Incense*, about a geisha and her daughter over a period of thirty years. Another was the re-make of the Mishima novel, *The Sound of Waves*, in which the innocence of the lovers is favorably contrasted with the experience of the world. In *Manji*, Masumura showed a love affair between girls and refused to falsify it, though he could not resist turning the picture into a bitter-sweet comedy in the final reels. *Onibaba* indicated that fear and jealousy is caused by the person feeling these emotions, but Kaneto Shindo made the message less attractive by descending into symbolism: the mother has a devil-mask which she can't get off her face, and when she does, it takes the face with it.

181

WOMAN OF THE DUNES is a definitive statement on responsibility, and consequently on the problem of evil. An innocent butterfly collector is made to live with a woman at the bottom of a sand pit. When he finally has a chance to escape, he refuses to. He has become interested in the way he has discovered for drawing water from the sand. Director Hiroshi Teshigahara filmed his parable in most realistic fashion, and by insisting upon this surface naturalism created a picture of several levels, only one of which was symbolic.

Woman of the Dunes, 1964, directed by Hiroshi Teshigahara, with Kyoko Kishida and Eiji Okada.

182

TOP LEFT: *The Assassin*, 1964, directed by Masahiro Shinoda, with Eiji Okada (left) and Ko Kimura (right). RIGHT: *Money Talks*, 1964, directed by Kon Ichikawa, with Shintaro Katsu (left) and Eiji Funakoshi. *Alone on the Pacific*, 1964, directed by Kon Ichikawa. CENTER LEFT: Ichikawa films a scene with Yujiro Ishihara. RIGHT: a scene with Ishihara.

TESHIGAHARA also made a very strong film about individual adaptation. This theme, in fact, has become a major one for Japanese films. Almost seventy years have elapsed since the days of the topknot and the double sword, but it has taken a number of wars and thousands of movies to begin to reflect this interest in the individual and his responsibilities. And this is what a great many good movies are about, including a great many Japanese movies. One was *The Assassin,* a period picture about a man who changes sides, not with the usual facility of the Japanese, but from conviction. A minor Ichikawa comedy, *Money Talks,* was about a single man who decides just where his responsibilities lie (with the gang rather than the police). A major Ichikawa film, *Alone on the Pacific,* was a brilliant film treatment of that true adventure story which galvanized Japan: a completely unknown Osaka boy sailed across the Pacific to San Francisco, alone and in a small ketch.

183

LEFT TOP AND CENTER: *Juvenile Delinquents*, 1964, directed by Kazuo Kawabe. *Hunger Straits*, 1965, directed by Tomu Uchida. BOTTOM LEFT: Junzaburo Ban (left) and Sachiko Hidari. RIGHT: Uchida directing.

184

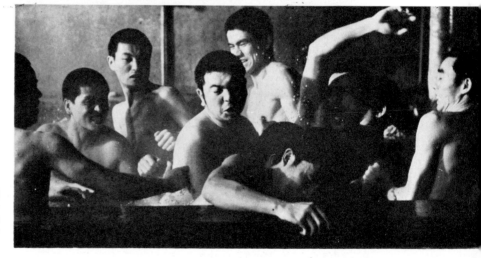

The Hoodlum Soldier, 1965, directed by Yasuzo Masumura. TOP: Masumura (left background) with Shintaro Katsu. CENTER: shooting scene. BOTTOM: the scene.

THE EXCELLENT *Juvenile Delinquents*, the debut film of Kazuo Kawabe, blamed not society but the boys and their teachers, while Uchida's *Hunger Straits* showed in a very straight-forward manner that a man's past (murder) may be thought to determine his actions, but that he himself is responsible for allowing this past to determine his future. Masumura's brutal comedy on wartime conditions in Manchuria, *The Hoodlum Soldier*, went the whole way. Two soldiers desert from the Imperial Army—and get away with it. The individual finally triumphs.

185

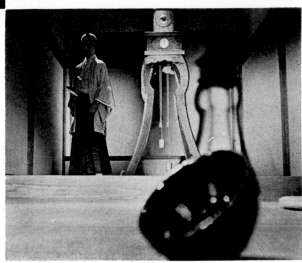

Kwaidan, 1965, directed by Masaki Kobayashi. TOP LEFT: Michiyo Aratama and Rentaro Mikuni. RIGHT: Katsuo Nakamura. CENTER LEFT: Tatsuya Nakadai (left) and Keiko Kishi. RIGHT: Noboru Nakaya.

THE INDIVIDUAL triumphs, in life as he does in film, and this is what any film history, any history at all would indicate, since that is the direction of our times and of our art. At the same time, our past predicates what we will become: we may celebrate our past and its continuance into the present; or we may affirm ourselves, the individual that we have become.

Throughout the history of Japanese film the movement between these poles has been apparent since before the first of the *Loyal Forty-seven Ronin*. One of the indications of the vitality of Japanese cinema is that it continues.

Kobayashi's *Kwaidan* is an evocation of the past which is also an excursion into that common unconscious which is peopled with demons and ghosts as well as kings and heroes. The floating world floats on and retribution strikes. One is the victim of a force larger than oneself, but since this force is life itself, its terrors are mitigated. Things go as they must.

186

Red Beard, 1965, directed by Akira Kurosawa. Scenes with Toshiro Mifune and Yuzo Kayama. TOP: Kayama (left) and Mifune.

In *Red Beard*, Kurosawa makes the opposite and equally valid statement that you are what you find it within yourself to be. A doctor teaches his young student the true meaning of dedication, of responsibility, to yourself and others. During this spiritual crisis which is the story of the film, Kurosawa indicates that you should turn your back upon this inevitable floating world, that it is no concern of yours. It does not dominate you; you dominate it.

That both statements should be equal is no paradox. Rather, these are opposite sides of the same thing and both are equally "true." Their apparent polarity is, after all, only apparent. And this becomes visible in Japan, a country where extremes meet and where the seeming incompatible are discovered to be one.

JAPANESE films indicate this in a way that no other contemporary Japanese art does or can. It is for this reason that the cinema is—in Japan more than in some other countries—a true mirror. It mirrors this audience, and its change reflects a like change. From the early and abiding interest in nature, through the celebration of the past indicated in the period film, through the identification with others as seen in the *shomin-geki*, through the postwar affirmation of the individual, the history of the Japanese film is also the history of Japanese popular thought. This does not argue for any concept as limited as that of progress. Rather it reflects the fortuitously occurring, the marvelously changing, the miraculous renewing, which becomes a part of film because it is all of life.

188

This index lists, in addition to proper names, etc., all of the film titles mentioned in both English and Japanese. It also gives various alternate English titles by which some films are known. The credits for the photos are also given here, directly behind the page entry upon which the photo appears. I am grateful to those persons, companies, and associations through whose courtesy I reproduce these photographs, and am indebted in particular to Hisamitsu Noguchi, the Tokutaro Osawa Estate, Junichiro Tanaka and Michio Matsuda of the Musei Eiga Kanshokai (Society for the Preservation and Enjoyment of Silent Films). I am also very grateful to Yoshihiro Hiranuma for his great help in properly transcribing names into romanized Japanese.

189

190

191

194

195

198

199